What Were They Thinking?

Marketing Lessons I've Learned from
over 80,000 New-Product
Innovations and Idiocies

Robert M. McMath
and Thom Forbes

TIMES BUSINESS

RANDOM HOUSE

Library of Congress Cataloging-in-Publication Data

McMath, Robert M.
What *were* they thinking? : marketing lessons I've learned from
over 80,000 new-product innovations and idiocies /
Robert M. McMath and Thom Forbes. — 1st ed.
p.   cm.
Includes index.
ISBN 0-8129-2950-0 (acid-free paper)
1. New products—Marketing.
2. New products—Marketing—Case studies.
I. Title.
HF5415.153.M348   1998
658.8′02—dc21   97-20804

Random House website address: www.randomhouse.com

Printed in the United States of America on acid-free paper

9 8 7 6 5 4 3 2

First Edition

Book design by Robert C. Olsson

I dedicate this book to Jean Huber McMath,
my wife, without whom I would not be able to do
what I do, and to Charles E. Mittelstadt,
former director of CAS, the information facility
of the Interpublic Group of Companies, Inc.,
without whom I wouldn't be what I am.
—*R.M.M.*

*Those who cannot remember the past
are condemned to repeat it.*
—George Santayana

Failure is an opportunity.
—Lao-tzu

*You can't turn a sow's ear into a Veal Orloff, but
you can do something very good with a sow's ear.*
—Julia Child

ACKNOWLEDGMENTS

Many people shared their wisdom and support over the years. Our families gave us both, and did so with great patience and love. Our agent, Joel Fishman, realized the potential of this project, helped us shape the proposal, and got the deal. Our editor, John Mahaney, knew where he wanted us to go and made sure that we got there. His assistant, Eleanor Wickland, ably assisted us on the last leg of the journey.

We are also indebted to scores of people we've talked to over the years whose insights helped us immeasurably, although they may not agree with our conclusions. We will not single any out. We wish to acknowledge their contributions, along with those of the exceptional journalists with whom we once worked at *Adweek's Marketing Week*, with a long sweeping bow and a doff of Bob's vintage top hat.

CONTENTS

Contents

D

E

F

G

H

Contents

Contents

P

Q

R

S

T

Contents

INTRODUCTION

Some nights at quitting time, after my clients have returned to their hotel rooms and I need to wind down after a day of fielding questions, I wander around my New Products Showcase and Learning Center here in Ithaca, New York. I've lost track of precisely how many once-new products line my gunmetal gray shelves or are packed away in storage, but 80,000 is a good estimate. As I walk by them, I can't help but notice that there are a lot more fizzlers than sizzlers. Duds. Losers. Wipeouts. Bombs.

I don't mean to be glum.

I started to gather new products almost thirty years ago for the same reason that scholars collect books: so that I could learn from them and teach others in turn. I'm not a morbid man. I like laughter and people of good cheer. I believe that smart ideas triumph over adversity and that a well-thought-out strategy, pursued with vigor and honesty, will prevail in the marketplace.

Well, most of the time.

Now that I look back, it was inevitable that I would end up with the world's largest Library of Losers. Even the best marketers in the world, like great baseball players, get to first base less than 40 percent of the time. Far less. And home runs are rare indeed.

Campbell Soup Company is among the most successful marketers of this century, for example. Among the more than 270 examples of Campbell's soups in my collection, however, are quite a few clunkers. Campbell's Fresh Chef, a line of refrigerated soups, was a bomb. So was Campbell's Creamy Natural Soup. Microwave Chunky Soup failed, too, as did Comin' Home Real Soup and Recipe Mix. And let's not forget Campbell's Souper Combos, which flopped despite a $10 million ad blitz in its final year.

Any winning marketer will have a similar lineup of losers, in fact.

As I stroll about the showcase, I am tempted to speak to some of the products. I'm particularly drawn to the ones that should have made it but didn't.

"So what's a nice product like you doing in a place like this?" I want to ask.

Now don't write me off as wacky. I assure you that even though these products don't talk back, they have a lot to tell us.

Sometimes the name was awful. Or if the name was great, maybe it tasted horrible. Perhaps its advertising was so clever that nobody knew what it could really do. Or perhaps there was no advertising or promotion at all and it withered like fruit in a frost. Maybe it was too pricey for the marketplace. Or too cheap.

Anyone who ever sold lemonade as a kid knows how difficult it is to market a product. First you've got to convince the bankers (your parents) that you've got an idea that's worth backing. Then you've got to get the flavor right. Not too tart; not too sweet. You've got to decide at which corner to build your stand, well aware that some envious kid from the next block (who's inevitably bigger) is going to set up right in front of you. You need to decide what price to charge—and then have the guts to drop it when Sluggo undercuts you by a nickel. And you can't be bashful about collaring every friend and grown-up who ambles by. Hard sell or soft sell, barker's shout or engaging smile, you need to draw attention to yourself.

Alas, I can't tell you that Everything You Ever Needed to Know About Marketing You Learned at the Lemonade Stand. It's just not that simple. No lemonade entrepreneur I ever knew had to pay a slotting fee, worry about a competitor's $50 million advertising budget, or figure out office politics.

New products succeed when just about everything that needs to go right does go right. That's a tough assignment. But if you realistically examine your concepts at the outset, rigorously question your assumptions as you develop them, and remain flexible enough to make necessary adjustments when you run into snags and hitches, your odds for success will improve substantially.

I would also suggest that you expand your definition of success. You are, as far as I'm concerned, a successful new-product developer if you abandon ideas that are destined to fail. Sometimes you'll read the signs of failure on the drawing board. Other times you may go all the way to a market test before you're able to spot some flaw. I'm not suggesting that you backpedal on a gutsy idea or yank a product from distribution at the first sign of difficulty. It's easy to be a naysayer or nitpicker. You need to be bold to succeed. But you should never hesitate to kill an untenable product before its costs get out of hand.

Of course, you have to know what's tenable and what's not. That's where this book comes in.

If there's one thing I've learned during my years of collecting new products—innovations, idiosyncrasies, and idiocies alike—it's that the odds for *successful* marketing increase exponentially if you are aware of what has succeeded and failed in the past. There are more losers than winners on my shelves simply because that's the way it works in the real world. But the winners have stories to tell, too.

If we are ignorant about the mistakes of the past, we are indeed bound to repeat them. In consumer-product marketing, we'll also lose a lot of money in the process. On the other hand, we can make a lot of money by emulating the successes.

How hard is it to get all the elements right? About 5,000 engineers designed the Boeing 777, integrating more than four million parts into the aircraft. The 777 should be flying well into the twenty-first century. If you pay due attention to all the details, and ask all the smart questions, your task is considerably easier.

Please read on. I suspect you've passed the first crucible of successful new-product marketing: an unquenchable fire in the belly.

—*Robert M. McMath*

What Were They Thinking?

ABRACADABRA ...

... Poof! Now you see it. And now you don't.

That's the way it is with most new products.

Many more products were launched during the 1990s than ever before. Consider Marketing Intelligence Service's ProductScan figures for consumable items:

Category	1989	1990	1991	1992	1993	1994	1995	1996
Foods	7,019	9,020	8,061	8,159	8,077	10,854	10,816	11,072
Beverages	1,402	1,621	1,805	1,611	2,243	2,597	2,581	3,524
Health and Beauty	3,434	3,530	4,035	4,625	5,327	7,161	5,861	8,204
Household	557	921	829	786	790	704	829	785
Pet	480	381	443	451	464	377	315	467
Other	492	406	228	254	462	293	406	444
Total	13,384	15,879	15,401	15,886	17,363	21,986	20,808	24,496

There were nearly twice as many introductions in 1996 than there were in 1989.

The great majority of these products—which include new flavors, sizes, and shapes as well as concepts conjured out of thin air—will fail miserably. Just as they did in 1989. And in 1979. And in 1968, when I began to collect new products.

In the extremely competitive world of consumer marketing, eight out of ten new products are failures, according to the conventional wisdom. Some pundits claim that failure runs as high as 94 percent. And an analyst's report several years ago purported that only 1 out of every 671 new-product ideas ever makes it to market and hits its sales or profit target. (I say purported because I've never been able to get my hands on the actual report. But the depressing statistic seems to have taken on a life of its own among journalists and presenters at new-product conferences.)

Let's grant one glum fact at the outset: The statistical odds against new-product success are considerably more daunting than those you face at the blackjack table.

ALZHEIMER'S, CORPORATE

"Today is the first day of the rest of your life" is an excellent adage for addictive personalities or people who have been through an upsetting experience. It's a horrible way for businesses to operate. That's just what many companies are doing, however, whether intentionally or not.

One of my major themes in speeches is the importance of bringing an historical perspective to new-product development. In order to successfully produce tomorrow's products, you must be aware of what has already succeeded and failed. Sure, times change. Tastes come and go. Fashion is fleeting. And just because an idea failed yesterday doesn't mean that it will flop tomorrow. But unless you understand *why* the concept failed yesterday, odds are that you'll make the same mistakes again.

Companies today have a terrible perspective on the past. From the mailroom to the boardroom, employees have little clue about their brand's culture or heritage. Your colleagues and employees are collectively afflicted with Corporate Alzheimer's. I see evidence of it all the time.

High-ranking marketers from major corporations have been shocked to find products at our New Products Showcase that were extremely similar to ones they were developing. And the shock hasn't always come because of the similarity of the product itself. Visitors often find products they weren't aware of that were marketed by their own company.

Incidences of Corporate Alzheimer's have become near epidemic during the past dozen years as corporations have merged, purged, and downsized for competitive reasons. Two things have happened:

1. Since no one feels secure anymore, there is no sense of loyalty to a company outside of doing the best you can out of personal pride while you're employed by it. Employees, from marketing trainees who intend to skip out at the first attractive offer to hired-gun CEOs who were brought in to get the company in fighting trim, don't really care about traditions or corporate culture. Everybody's a short-termer. They not only couldn't care a whit about the past, but also don't think about the future one minute past the day they intend to leave the company.

2. Less talked about but just as critical, I believe, is that many of the people who have been pushed out of

our corporations are old-timers who rose through the ranks. Generally disparaged as "dead wood," these mid-level managers are the ones who have "been there, done that." Their lack of unbridled enthusiasm about every idea that comes down the pike can annoy young marketers on the move. The old-timers are often accused of failing "to get with the program," which leads to their being included on the corporate hit list. But their informed, dispassionate viewpoint is precisely why they're so valuable.

These veterans not only know what has been tried in the past, they also know what has been bandied about and scrapped for good reason. They know the skinny on why a project failed—for example, lack of support from top management or an inept project leader—which can be quite different from the official explanation. They were privy to hush-hush development meetings for which there are no formal records. They know where the bodies are buried, what questions to raise, and who to turn to for assistance.

But these mid-level executives are no longer hidden away in windowless offices, as they once were, waiting for the right challenge to rejuvenate their enthusiasm and careers. They're pensioned off in a Sunbelt condo somewhere, or are working for the competition. (Hint: Bring these grizzled veterans back as per-diem consultants. Pay them whatever they ask; they'll save you much more in the long run.)

Because of Corporate Alzheimer's, we see a lot more products come to test markets that are nearly carbon copies of ideas or concepts that failed in the past.

For example, Cool Mint Listerine toothpaste is not the first toothpaste that Warner-Lambert, the manufacturer of Listerine, has marketed using the venerable mouthwash's name. Its first attempt failed, I believe, because consumers think of Listerine as having a bad taste. Consumers accept Listerine mouthwash's antiseptic taste because decades of advertising have convinced them that "Listerine kills the germs that cause bad breath." Listerine tastes so bad, they reason, that it must knock off germs with the vengeance of a cold-blooded killer. But consumers won't accept toothpaste that sounds like it tastes bad, whether it actually does or not. Obviously, that's why Listerine has given its "new" toothpaste a mint flavor.

This is a case where a powerful brand name gets in the way of the message the new product wants to convey. It's more important to consumers that toothpaste prevents cavities and gingivitis than prevents bad breath. The Listerine mouthwash heritage is that it tastes bad but it's good for you. Perhaps Warner-Lambert got cocky because of the moderate success of its Cool Mint mouthwash. That's simply a flavor extension, however. People expect different things from their mouthwash and toothpaste, and the company would have been better served if it had established a new brand for the paste. Consumers didn't warm up to Listerine brand toothpaste in 1979, and I doubt that they will today.

Corporate Alzheimer's has other symptoms. Companies without veterans from the trenches of yesterday's marketing wars are oblivious to even broader strategic lessons than the failure of a single product.

Right now, for example, a battle is raging in the body-wash business. It's very reminiscent of the fight that began in January 1980, when Minnetonka, Inc., a small manufacturer of scented specialty soaps, took its innovative Softsoap into national distribution after two years of testing.

Softsoap was the first liquid hand-and-body cleanser designed to compete with regular-priced bar soap. Minnetonka's major innovation was a pump dispenser through which the soap flowed easily. It was a smash hit, and the soap industry was delirious with expectations. Dozens of me-too competitors hit the market. Within eighteen months, liquid soaps accounted for 8.4 percent of the personal soap business. Even *Business Week* got into a lather. An article asked: "Is the Bar of Soap Washed Up?" Some analysts were predicting that liquid soaps would capture as much as 40 percent of the market.

Most of the smaller competitors didn't last long, and Minnetonka survived only until some giant soap brands—Jergens Liquid Soap (then owned by American Brands) and P&G's Ivory Liquid—entered the fray and turned the market into a price-and-coupon battlefield.

In the mid-1980s, Colgate-Palmolive acquired Softsoap. Through the late eighties and early nineties, Ivory Liquid, Liquid Dial, and Softsoap battled it out for the lead in market share. Product developments such as the antibacterial soap introduced by Liquid Dial in 1989 periodically sparked renewed enthusiasm for the category, but it never came close to capturing 40 percent of the market. At its best, it had about 12 percent.

The reason the liquid-soap bubble burst has more to do with the nature of the American consumer than with anything else.

Think about all the soap and shampoo commercials you've seen. What's the one element that sticks out? Thick, foamy lather. Bubbles galore. Americans associate luscious bubbles with the cleansing process. But liquid soaps are made from detergent material. They do not foam in the shower unless something like a washcloth is used to make them lather. Many women use washcloths in the shower, but most men prefer to wash with their bare hands. Liquid soap did not fulfill its promise as a category because Americans weren't about to change their bathing habits to accommodate the new product, and research showed that as much as 70 percent of bar soap was used in the shower.

In 1994, Kao launched Jergens Body Shampoo in the United States. The Japanese conglomerate had acquired the Jergens brand in the late 1980s. Packaged with a sponge, which generates more lather than a washcloth, Body Shampoo was the first of the new wave of liquid washes and gels designed exclusively for the shower. Competitors rushed to market. P&G introduced an Oil of Olay body-wash line. Lever weighed in with both its Caress and Dove brands, and Dial developed its own version. All of these me-too body-wash kits come with a puff that, like the sponge, creates lather.

When Kao launched Body Shampoo, a company executive told me that it would spend $110 million over three years in advertising and promotion. I thought it was crazy to spend that kind of money on a product that required Americans to change their bathing habits, and said so in an article I wrote for *Brand Marketing* magazine. Jergens executives met with my editor to protest. If the body shampoo was such a bad idea, they asked, why were so many other companies coming to market with similar products? Well, if faulty ideas weren't frequently copied by other companies, even companies that are generally very smart, the New Products Showcase wouldn't contain nearly as many losing products as it does.

Jergens Body Shampoo isn't a bad idea or product, actually; it just isn't worth a $110 million marketing investment. And it needs a few positioning tweaks. Yes, Jergens—and its competitors—is supplying an implement that makes a liquid cleanser lather in the shower, and those bubbles assure Americans that they're getting clean. I don't think men will use the sponges or puffs, however. Similarly, you could flood the market with inexpensive cricket bats, but the British sport would never supplant baseball in the hearts of American males. They are creatures of habit and upbringing.

Worse yet, perhaps, the name "Body Shampoo" is all wrong for American women. They associate *"shampoo"* with hair, not with skin. It's a monumental mistake to suggest to an American woman that she has a hairy body. Even subtly. One aspect of the feminist movement that never caught on was letting underarm, leg, and facial hair grow. It may be natural, but it's not fashionable. Women spend a bundle on various products that get rid of body hair; they don't want to even think about cleansing it.

Bathing is an entirely different ritual in Japan and Europe than it is in the United States. Body shampoo may be an excellent idea for those markets. But the marketing executives associated with the American launch of Jergens Body Shampoo should have had the historical sense to realize that the main problem with liquid soap in the shower was not so much that it didn't lather as that it required consumers to change the way they bathed to make it lather. So does their new product.

They also should have understood that Americans deeply believe that what's appropriate for their tresses is not appropriate for their skin. There have been several attempts to market combination hair-and-body washing products over the years, in fact, but all have failed. No wonder. Marketers spend more than a half billion dollars annually in advertising that differentiates the cleansing properties of various soaps, shampoos, and cleaners. That's why I buy a deodorant soap and my wife buys one that moisturizes her skin.

I see dozens of players in the body-wash market today, just as there were in the liquid-soap business in the 1980s. My historical perspective tells me that perhaps three of the top brands will survive by pouring a lot of money into continually improving their products and by keeping them in the minds of consumers through expensive advertising. So will a few specialty brands from smaller companies that limit their distribution and marketing and are satisfied with a few hundred thousand dollars in annual sales. All of the rest of the brands are battling for a market that is nowhere near as bountiful as they wish it to be. They will become part of the ever-expanding case history that illustrates one of the most vital points I can make to you: Those who ignore the marketing mistakes of the past will not only repeat them, they will lose a lot of money in the process.

ADVERTISING AGENCIES

A good advertising campaign is simple to execute.

So is chipping away at all the excess marble until a beautiful sculpture emerges.

Don't kid yourself. You can't do it alone.

Before all the mergers and acquisitions of the 1980s shook up long-standing relationships, agencies played a greater role in developing their clients' products than they do today. Marketers must again include their agencies as full partners in their business instead of treating them as mere suppliers of spectacular thirty-second videos and splashy magazine ads.

If you don't have an advertising agency, get one. It should be involved with all of your development and strategy meetings from the time that you have a viable new product concept.

Don't let the agency people tell you what they think you want to hear. Make them prod and challenge you. When they start creating the actual campaign, prod and challenge them. All this prodding and challenging will result in fewer mistakes. It may even convince you that your product is not viable. So be it.

Don't let the agency assign a bunch of green kids to your account just because it's a new product. You need people with enough perspective and guts to tell you when you're about to make mistakes that have been made before. Or that you should try an approach that worked for a client in an entirely different category. Or that the images or positioning that has worked for your other brands are not appropriate for the product you are developing.

Sure, agencies cost money. But if you use their people correctly, you're not just buying a slick commercial, print ad, or Web site. You are tapping into a broad range of experience that can save you from your own blind enthusiasm. Believe me, nobody can spot worthless hype faster than a good advertising person.

ADVERTISING 101

It's as important to not get your advertising wrong as it is to get it right. Bad positioning or the wrong image can kill a new product as quickly as anything that's inherently wrong with the product itself.

Does the name Gablinger's ring a bell?

How about Miller Lite?

Gablinger's could have been Miller Lite, but it got the positioning wrong.

Gablinger's was introduced in 1967 as a "low-calorie" beer. A diet beer. A beer for moderation. A beer that fat people could drink and not gain as much weight as they would with "normal" beer. In other words, a beer for namby-pambies.

Heavy beer drinkers—and most beer is bought by heavy drinkers—are not the sort of consumers who care about washboard abs. They responded much more positively to Miller Lite's positioning of "less filling" five years later. First, "less filling" means you can drink more. And one-third the calories means you can have two more cans and call it even, right? Miller Lite was, in fact, "everything you ever wanted in a beer . . . and less." Indeed, heavy beer drinkers knew what they wanted in a beer. A buzz. The tag line implied that they could get it.

Some of the most macho men in America—sports greats like Dick Butkus, Boog Powell, and John Madden—pushed Miller Lite. They were men of great girth and, as it turned out, great mirth. They had a rip-roaring time downing brews, oblivious to their rotundity. Show me a man concerned about his waistline and I'll show you a poor prospect for serious beer drinking.

Miller Lite made the world safe for other light beers, such as Bud Light, Coors Light, and numerous regional brands. The category has been one of the most successful food and beverage innovations of the past twenty-five years. Often, the successful positioning of one product can open up the door to consumer acceptance of an entire category.

Steve Case, the entrepreneurial CEO of America Online, was ecstatic when well-funded Prodigy Interactive Services mounted a mass-market advertising campaign in 1992. He knew that Prodigy's widespread TV commercials and print ads would introduce millions of unenlightened consumers to the wonders of online technology.

At the time, Prodigy had 860,000 members; America Online had only 181,000. But America Online possessed superior content and technology. Consumers who were initially seduced by Prodigy's advertising switched to America Online once they realized that it offered a better product. By 1996, America Online had eight million members while Prodigy was struggling to survive. Heavy advertising and good positioning will always attract trial users. But all the advertising in the world won't sustain an inferior brand.

If you can't get your positioning right, at least don't get it wrong—and back it up with a decent product.

AT WHAT PROFIT?

When the gunslingers of the Old West won a shoot-out on Main Street, they didn't always walk away into the setting sun, the way they do in Hollywood movies. Often as not, they'd get hauled off to jail to await the hangman's noose.

Some new products are like that. You may win the gunfight. But at what cost? More to the point, at what profit?

How large your market needs to be is certainly a relative question. If you're Budweiser, with a huge amount of capital tied up in breweries across the country, relationships with more than 900 wholesalers to maintain, and with a commitment to spending about $100 million a year to advertise your brand, you need to sell an awful lot of suds to many millions of people. If you want to compete directly against Anheuser-Busch's Budweiser, Bud Light, Busch, or Busch Light brands, you'll need to make a similar investment in equipment and image-making.

Anheuser-Busch's total sales, which include other

divisions, are around $12 billion each year. Its margin is generally in the 5 percent to 8 percent range. I've got a few stocks that yield better than that. But my net income from them is measured in the thousands of dollars, not the hundreds of millions. And my salary is considerably less than the $2 million or so that August A. Busch III takes home as chairman and president of his own show.

If you have more modest expectations than Anheuser-Busch, you might join the ranks of the about 700 microbreweries around the country that generally sell premium ale or lager within a limited geographical area. Revenues are certainly much less than they are at the huge breweries, but the margins must be enticing. There were only about 75 microbreweries in the country in 1990.

Microbrewers generally produce less than 15,000 barrels a year. Some microbrewed beers, in fact, are sold only within the confines of the brewery itself in a subgroup called brew pubs. Others have expanded into local stores or restaurants. Still others, such as Anchor Brewing of San Francisco, have expanded outside their primary market and are considered regional specialty brewers. And Boston-based Samuel Adams has developed an even larger following across the country.

Microbreweries have tapped into several trends. First, the interest in specialty and ethnic foods with intriguing flavors is growing, and the microbrewed beers have a more distinctive taste than the mass-produced versions. It's the same difference as that between a bagged loaf of white bread and a freshly baked loaf of multigrained cracked wheat. Second, many people are drinking more moderately, but they are drinking "better." That means they are willing to spend the same amount of money on one beer with dinner that they used to spend for two on the way home from work.

As hot as microbreweries had become by the mid-1990s, they represented only about 1 percent of the $50 billion in annual beer sales. The most optimistic analysts predicted that they'd capture, at best, 5 percent to 10 percent of the market within the next decade. Is that a large enough pie for your product? It depends on how large an appetite you bring to the table. Entrepreneurs only need to feed themselves and a few others; larger companies must worry about legions of hungry employees and shareholders.

Sometimes products are killed before they're launched because it is clear that they are going to be nothing but a drain on resources. Good business means balancing risk-taking with prudence. It sometimes takes more courage to kill a product that's going nowhere fast than it does to sustain it.

H.J. Heinz, for example, showed guts in pulling the plug on Help, a liquid fruit-flavored beverage concentrate that it developed for several years in the early 1970s. Heinz never said exactly why it gave up, but I was told it determined that Help could do no more than $10 million in annual business. That amount—a tidier sum twenty-five years ago than it is today—just wasn't enough revenue for Heinz. Perhaps it feared that companies with more expertise in beverage marketing would come in with me-too products and slice up the pie further. Perhaps its business model projected

$11 million in expenses. I do know that other marketers thought enough of the product that they wanted to buy it, but Heinz turned away all inquiries.

Even products that are huge successes from a marketing standpoint are sometimes losers at the cash register. When the accountants add up the numbers, all they see is red. So, too, do shareholders. In today's environment, it's corporate suicide to continue to market a money loser or a low-margin product. However, shareholders and management sometimes lose sight of the tangential benefits of products that may not make a lot of money but nonetheless add value to a company.

Jell-O Pudding Pops are a perfect example. When General Foods decided to enter the freezer case in the 1980s, it was taking a huge financial gamble with a brand name that had been a solid performer throughout the twentieth century. It was cheap to buy but a lot cheaper to make and market. In short, it was a mature brand that was a very simple formula for making money hand over fist. Truth was, though, Jell-O's image had lost its pizzazz. It was an old standby in the cupboard, an easy-to-prepare dessert from another era. Sales were slipping.

Jell-O Pudding Pops went into test in 1979. The product was a new direction for the brand in two ways. First, it suggested that Jell-O was contemporary and fun to eat. Second, it launched General Foods into the frozen desserts category.

Pudding Pops were backed by a huge advertising campaign featuring Jell-O's avuncular spokesman, Bill Cosby. Sales nearly hit $100 million during its first year in national distribution. Before long, General Foods introduced lines of Gelatin Pops and frozen Fruit Bars. Within five years, its frozen novelties business went from $0 to $300 million, and Pudding Pops was the leading brand in the category. If you look in the freezer case today, however, you won't find the Jell-O name at all.

Other marketers didn't let General Foods rest on its laurels. Everything from Snickers bars to the Trix cereal brand also entered the freezer case, which squeezed prices as well as space. General Foods also discovered that frozen foods require a lot more attention than packages of Jell-O powder. Competitors who were already making regular deliveries to the freezer case found it a lot more efficient to replenish supplies than General Foods did. Despite the high sales figures, the company eventually decided that there wasn't enough margin in the Pudding Pops business to make it worthwhile.

From a marketing standpoint, Pudding Pops and its siblings were raging successes. From a financial standpoint, they were bombs—at least on the surface. Look a little deeper, though, and you'll discover one of those tangential benefits that CEOs find difficult to quantify when they are facing shareholders.

Pudding Pops rejuvenated the Jell-O brand. One executive who ran the business said that subsequent popular extensions, such as Jell-O Jigglers, would not have been possible if Pudding Pops had not introduced an element of fun in the brand's marketing. The positioning that Jell-O is fun to eat remains the core message of the brand's advertising today.

For every company that finds $300 million in sales does not provide sufficient return on investment, however, there are thousands of entrepreneurs who build much smaller businesses that are perfectly suited to their talents, temperament, and definition of a reasonable profit (See *Fire in the Belly*).

B

BENEFITS, NOT FEATURES

The benefits of a product are all-important—I should say that the *perceived* benefits are all-important. Calvin Klein isn't selling perfume. He's selling sex. But this is a principle that also applies in more nuts-and-bolts categories. I once saw it written, for example, that consumers don't walk into a hardware store to buy a $1/4$-inch drill bit. They want a $1/4$-inch hole. As a marketer, you must make the concept of a $1/4$-inch hole synonymous with your brand of drill bit. Year after year, for example, Coca-Cola's advertising drummed variations of the word *refresh*—refreshes, refreshing, refreshed, refreshment—into the American psyche. Coke owned a benefit that almost all of us feel a need for from time to time.

One of the most common mistakes that marketers make is that they communicate the features of a product rather than the benefits. Imagine the results if Coke's advertising slogan had been "the pause that's cold and wet" rather than "the pause that refreshes."

A feature is something that the folks in the research and development department get excited about. A benefit is something that excites the buyer. Features are for dweebs and bean counters; benefits are for consumers and buyers. A feature is what a product does; a benefit is what a product does *for me.*

British comedian John Cleese made a training film for salespeople that illustrates the folly of trying to sell features rather than benefits. Cleese portrays a surgeon who is explaining an upcoming procedure to an anxious patient lying in a hospital bed.*

"Have I got an operation for you," Cleese begins eagerly. "Only three incisions and an Anderson slash, a Ridgeway stubble-side fillip and a standard dormer slip! Only five minutes with the scalpel; only thirty stitches! We can take out up to five pounds of your insides, have you back in your hospital bed in seventy-five minutes flat, and we can do ten of them in a day.

"Shall I put you down for three?"

Cleese's surgeon has a demonstrably superior product. He's talking to a customer who is interested in what it could do for him. But all the customer discovers is that after a gory surgical procedure, he'll be right back where he started. In the hospital bed. What he wants to know is when he'll be playing golf again.

Put your customers on the golf course.

BESMIRCHING YOUR GOOD NAME

Can you imagine the reaction of a congregation if its minister announced that he embraced the values of sex, drugs, and rock and roll? Can you imagine the reaction of Pearl Jam fans if lead singer Eddie Vedder renounced loud music?

---

*So You Want to Be a Success at Selling—Part 2, © Video Arts Ltd., Videocassette. Produced by Margaret Tree, directed by Peter Robinson.

The value of a brand is its good name, which it earns over time. People become loyal to it. They trust it to deliver a consistent set of attributes.

Don't squander this trust by attaching your good name to something totally out of character.

Millions of Americans love Frito-Lay's salty snacks. But Frito-Lay products have never been known to quench thirst. In fact, they make people's tongues feel like swaths of felt. That's why PepsiCo, which was the parent company of the brand, made a terrible mistake in naming a new powdery refreshment Frito-Lay Lemonade.

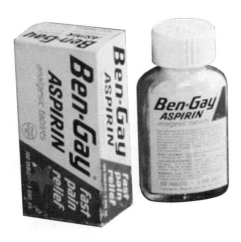

When you hear Ben-Gay Aspirin, don't you immediately think of the way that Ben-Gay cream sears your skin? Can you imagine swallowing it?

Louis Sherry No Sugar Added Gorgonzola Cheese Dressing was everything that Louis Sherry, known for its rich candies and ice cream, shouldn't be: sugarless, cheese, and salad dressing.

Cracker Jack Cereal, Smucker's Premium Ketchup,

Fruit of the Loom Laundry Detergent, and Noxema Solid Anti-Perspirant Deodorant were other misbegotten attempts to stretch a good name.

A good brand name stands for something vibrant. You can suck the life out of it by attaching it to a new product that stands for something totally different (see *Fooling with Your Cash Cow*).

BOOM, BOOM, BOOM

That's me, beating my favorite drum: The more new products we produce, the less innovative they seem to be.

I began to notice that products were becoming less innovative at an alarming rate in the mid-1980s. To prove my hunch, several associates and I developed an Innovation Index to measure whether each new product shown at trade shows or launched into the marketplace actually offered consumers a meaningful difference from existing brands.

To establish a base, we assigned an Innovation Rating to every product we were aware of that had been identified as new from 1980 forward. To qualify as innovative, a product had to offer consumers a significant new or added benefit in one of the following five areas: positioning, packaging, formulation, technology, or previously unmet market need.

According to the Innovation Index we developed, only 18.9 percent of the new products in 1986 could be considered innovative. We thought that was a startling number, even lower than we anticipated. By 1989, however, the percentage had dropped to 13.4 percent. The following year it plummeted to 8.4 percent as a national recession took hold. By 1993, the figure was down to about 5.1 percent, although it has been inching its way back up and reached 7.2 percent in 1995.*

Here are the five criteria we developed, along with examples of products that qualified, and did not qualify, as innovative when the measures were applied:

1. Is the product positioned to new users or usage?

Rembrandt Low-Abrasion Whitening Toothpaste for Kids, for example, represented a new positioning for whitening toothpastes and was therefore considered innovative. Previously, teeth whiteners had been pitched to older consumers with yellowing teeth or to smokers.

On the other hand, Topol Smoker's Toothpaste had already been in distribution for five years when Zact Smoker's Toothpaste tried to carve a presence in the same market.

2. Is there new packaging that provides a consumer benefit?

Smucker's Beverage Division introduced a six-ring carrier to its line of fruit-based beverages that was made of pressed biodegradable fibers instead of the plastic found on most soft drink multipacks. This packaging innovation provided an environmental benefit that's important to many consumers.

---

*The Innovation Index was developed with the help of Ed Ogiba, who is now president of Group EFO in Norwalk, Connecticut, while I was chairman of Marketing Intelligence Service. I founded MIS in 1968, sold it to a division of Ogilvy & Mather in 1983, and worked with it as chairman until 1988. MIS, which is in Naples, New York, continues to issue a yearly Innovation Index, which it markets under the name ProductScan.

In the early 1980s, Colgate-Palmolive introduced a powdered detergent called Fresh Start that was packaged inside a clear plastic bottle. Innovative, again. After a while, Stanson Detergents came out with a box of concentrate that featured a clear cutout on the front panel through which the consumer could see the detergent. There was a bottle outline printed on the panel that carried the slogan "No bottle inside, that's why you save!" The package certainly looked different from other detergent packages. But the clear cutout existed solely to position the product against Fresh Start. There was no perceptible benefit to the consumer.

3. Is value added through a new formulation?

Soaps and shampoos have come in many scents and varieties over the years, but St. Ives Swiss Formula Vanilla Shampoo was, in my experience, the first toiletries product to use a vanilla scent. Because scent is so important to the health and beauty care category, it was clearly an innovative product.

The cinnamon spice version of Accents Potpourri Glass Cleaner, on the other hand, was little more than a gimmick. The world did not need a glass cleaner that smelled like a mouthwash. Since no value was added to the glass cleaner, the product, different as it was, was not innovative.

4. Is there a technological introduction?

Salem Preferred Menthol cigarettes were manufactured with a proprietary paper technology that purportedly made the odor of a burning cigarette less

offensive to nonsmokers. Even though it was a misguided idea because it addressed the wrong market (see
Ice Cubes to Cocker Spaniels), it was technologically
innovative.

General Mills' Mrs. Bumby's Potato Chips, however, were nothing more than a copycat version of
Procter & Gamble's Pringles Potato Chips. Mrs.
Bumby's chips came stacked in a circle around the
edge of a resealable "Flavor-Pack Bowl" instead of
being stacked in a canister as Pringles were. The presentation was really the only major difference between
the two products; the production technology was basically the same. It was not innovative.

5. Does the product open up a new market for the category?

Arizona Iced Tea Freez-A-Pops was probably the
first beverage, and was certainly the first tea, to become a freeze-and-squeeze ice. It was a clever way to
introduce the taste of tea to kids who, on a hot day, love
to squeeze slushy ice crystals into their mouths.

Three Musketeers ice cream bars were not innovative because other candy bars were in the freezer case
before it.

More than nine out of ten consumable products
launched in the mid-1990s offered absolutely nothing
new to the consumer. More than eight out of ten new
products fail. You don't need to be a statistician to
realize there's a correlation between the two numbers.

I'm not saying that you *absolutely have to be* innovative to succeed. A Three Musketeers ice cream bar
offers a different taste than a Snickers does, after all.

But the Number One killer of new products is, without any doubt, Me-Tooism (see *Me-Too Madness*).

BUY-THIS-IF-YOU'RE-A-LOSER SCHOOL OF MARKETING

Don't be fooled by the success of the *Complete Dummy's Guide to . . .* line of books. People usually don't buy products that remind them of their shortcomings.

Gillette's For Oily Hair Only shampoo flopped because people did not want to confess that they had greasy hair. People will use products that discreetly say "for oily hair" or "for sensitive skin" in small print on containers that are otherwise identical to the regular product. But they do not want to be hit over the head with reminders that they are overweight, have bad breath, sweat too much, or are elderly. Nor do they wish to advertise their faults and foibles to other people by carrying such products in their grocery carts.

Emphasize the positive in your name. Obfuscate the negative.

Gillette must have learned its lesson. It named its best-selling disposable razor Good News, which is certainly a perky way to describe the benefits of scraping a blade across your face in the morning.

CHORD OF FAMILIARITY

Some products are radically different from the products, services, or experiences that consumers normally purchase. Too radically different. They fail because consumers don't relate to them. They do not strike what I call the "Chord of Familiarity."

Sometimes the idea for a product is sound, but consumers just don't have enough time to get to know it. People are naturally suspicious of products that don't look, taste, feel, or smell like what they're used to, just as they are wary of people who act differently. If you want to succeed with a product that's radically different, you've either got to keep it on the market long enough for people to get comfortable with it—Pringles Potato Chips are a good example—or you've got to create a Chord of Familiarity through great advertising, as Volkswagen did with its Beetle.

You can tell (at least I can) that some innovative products are doomed as soon as you hear their names. Toaster Eggs. Cucumber Antiperspirant Spray. Health-Sea Sea Sausage.

Other innovative ideas have been victims of a brand's past success.

For example, Nabisco's Oreo Little Fudgies, a confectionery product with a chocolate coating meant to compete with candy, sounds like a natural. But for many years Nabisco has encouraged people to pull apart Oreo cookies and lick out the filling. It's very messy to open an Oreo with a chocolate coating, however, so Oreo Little Fudgies struck a discordant note with consumers.

In the same vein, many kids grew up mixing Kool Aid powder with water. Kool Aid Kool Shots Concentrate, which was a liquid, took the familiar product into a different category. In liquid form, the potential for a spill is more likely. In fact, except in a few instances, such as Campbell's standard red-and-white line of soups, people prefer their concentrated foods to be in powdered form, whether it's salad dressings, sauce mixes, or other lines of soup.

Other innovative ideas, such as Sweater Fresh, just go against the grain. The idea was that instead of sending a sweater to the dry cleaner or putting it in the washing machine, you sprayed it with Sweater Fresh and put it in the dryer for a few minutes. But consumers could not relate to this claim. Even if Sweater Fresh removed odors, how could it possibly make the garment clean? Consumers believe that if a piece of clothing smells unpleasant, it's too dirty to wear, and they had no familiarity with getting clothing clean in the dryer.

Finally, some innovative ideas are fine in particular markets but won't work in others. Baker's Select Bread Mix, a yeast product, has been quite successful in the United Kingdom, where some people still make bread from scratch. In the United States, people generally make "homemade" bread from a mix, and almost all of the mixes already have yeast in them. Baker's Select did not hit the right note with American consumers.

People like to leave a musical humming the tune. If your new product does not strike a Chord of Familiarity with them, it will flop on the Great Fluorescent Way otherwise known as the local supermarket.

COMMUNICATE CLEARLY

Someone once gave me three rules for making a successful speech:

1. Tell the audience what you're going to tell them.
2. Tell them.
3. Tell them what you told them.

In the same manner, you must very clearly present your new product to consumers. Never assume that they know why they should use the product, how they should prepare or operate it, or what its purpose may be. Be very explicit in your packaging. Make sure that instructions and directions cannot be misinterpreted. Packaging is no place for subtlety. You cannot be too clear.

Let me illustrate this point by asking you to imagine yourself in a scene of great triumph, tinged with a hint of romance.

Let's say you've just signed a deal that is going to put your new product into national distribution. Your spouse is equally ecstatic after spending an afternoon playing golf with prospective clients. The kids are attending choir practice, out of your hair for the evening. It's the perfect time for a candlelit dinner for just the two of you. But who has time to prepare a gourmet feast anymore?

"Hmmmmm," you say to yourself. "Why don't I prepare that package of Wine & Dine I picked up at the supermarket for a special occasion just like this?"

You toss the rotini macaroni in a pot of boiling water, throw the sauce mix into a frying pan, add some chopped beef. Voila! Ten minutes later you're sitting down at the dining room table, proposing a toast to everlasting *amore*. The rims of the wineglasses touch your lips simultaneously . . .

"Ptoooey!" you spit.

"Yuck!" your spouse agrees.

Face scrunched in disgust, you grab the bottle. Instead of a year of vintage, you discover that the wine has been "salted and spiced for this recipe." And under that, you discover that this Chianti "is not for beverage use." Only then do you realize that the wine was supposed to be mixed into the sauce, not rolled on the tongue.

I dramatize for effect, but that's what I imagine happened time and again to people who brought home Heublein's Wine & Dine a couple of decades ago. It was sort of an upscale Hamburger Helper, which was just gaining popularity at the time. The packaging was very attractive and enticing. The pasta was on one side of the box; the other, which was cut out, showed a bottle of Chianti. The wine was supposed to be used as an ingredient in the sauce mix, but this was not made clear on the front of the package. And because Heublein was known as a wine company, not a food company, many people just assumed that it was for drinking, not for cooking. The wine was salted so that it could be sold in supermarkets in states where wine sales are not permitted in retail stores.

Prepared properly, Wine & Dine was a tasty meal that was reasonably priced. It could have succeeded if its name and packaging clearly communicated what the product was instead of inadvertently misleading many consumers.

As smart and discriminating as your consumers may be, you can never rely on their common sense. Be very explicit about exactly how your product should be used, or not used. The more information you provide, in fact, the more reasons people will have to buy it. Many sauces can be used in ways that are not immediately apparent to run-of-the-pepper-mill cooks, for example. Enlighten them. If your Hot Tamale Sauce can be used to liven up an egg salad as well as barbecued ribs, say so. There's only so much room on a label, but you can print enticing recipes in advertisements or booklets. The more uses people find for your product, the quicker they'll use it up. Translation: increased sales.

On the other hand, consumers sometimes do just the opposite of what you intend or make assumptions that you wish they hadn't. Executives at Planters nuts told me a story that springs to mind every time someone thinks that I overestimate the need for clarity.

A few years ago, Planters began to market its Fresh Roasted Peanuts in a package that looked like a vacuum brick-pack of coffee. Planters hoped that the association of fresh roasted would carry over from coffee to peanuts. Did it ever!

The outer surface of the package was very bumpy, and the label was difficult to read under harsh supermarket lighting. All of a sudden, irate supermarket managers started calling Planters wanting to know who was going to pay to have their coffee-grinding machines cleaned. Shoppers, the managers reported, were transporting the peanut packages from the snack shelf to the coffee aisle and running the contents through the grinders. They thought it was a new brand of coffee.

Other products give instructions that seem counterintuitive. To this day, I wonder about Maxwell House Brewed Coffee. It came in a 48-ounce container that looked like a milk carton. There was a screw top on the side of the gable so that it could be poured without the usual struggle to open the gable. The directions merely instructed the user to pour the coffee out and heat it up in a microwave. If you've got access to a microwave, however, chances are that you're also able to brew a fresh pot of hot coffee. And if you don't want to go to all that bother, or only want a single cup, you certainly can heat up a mug of water and add a soluble mix. There was no need for an alternative way to prepare hot coffee.

Ready-to-drink iced coffee that the consumer could pour straight into a glass, on the other hand, would have made sense. If this was what Maxwell House had in mind, it should have explicitly said so on the carton. There was plenty of room to stress the product's freshness as well, but the only message the consumer received was of dubious value: how to heat the brew.

Assume not only that consumers won't know how to prepare your product but also that they won't understand how to use it.

CONVENIENCE: HOT BUTTON #1 FOR THE MILLENNIUM

If the consumer must chose between what's politically correct and what's expedient, the latter will win 90 percent of the time. Although people pay lip service to the environment (another Hot Button for the Millennium), they will pay a premium for a product that makes their lives easier.

Consumers buy single-serve cups of soup, breakfast cereals, or even dried mashed potatoes for various reasons. Some people live alone. Others live in large families where everybody is on a different schedule or likes different types of foods or flavors. Some people like the fact that the containers are easily transportable. All the reasons boil down to one word: convenience.

Convenience is anything that saves time. One-stop shopping. Electronic ordering of groceries. Home delivery. Mail-order clothing and gift shopping.

Convenience also can be delivered by offering a new way to open a package. Or a simpler way to seal it easily for safety reasons. Convenience is a new way to prepare food quickly. Or to package it, such as the salads that come bagged with the lettuce and carrots chopped up and the dressing in the pack. It is new take-out deli meals or retail operations that prepare "home-cooked" meals like Boston Market or Subway, which makes *fresh*, custom-made sandwiches right before your eyes.

There are many other ways that you can build convenience into your products. Convenience is:

- Easy transportation to stores
- Ample parking close to the destination
- A Laundromat that picks up, washes, folds, and delivers laundry to a home or office

- Twenty-four-hour ATM banking
- Prepaid phone cards
- Cellular phones

Time is one commodity that nobody, even a billionaire, has enough of. Any product, concept, or service that spares the consumer just one second of frustration—I'm thinking here of improving childproof caps that presently are also McMath-proof—will be as hot a button as you can push.

CULTURE SHOCK

Grubs are delicacies in some cultures, ants in others. But don't even think about it in the U.S.A. It makes me shudder to think that cats and turtles are eaten in Asia, yet I feel absolutely no compunction about digging into a juicy sirloin steak, an act that a Hindu would find repulsive.

I'll never forget a caller to a radio talk show I was a guest on a few years ago. In between the usual questions—"Whatever happened to Fizzies?"; "Why didn't biodegradable garbage bags make it?"—I usually attract a bunch of entrepreneurs who want to talk about their "can't-miss" products.

This caller had introduced a product called Rabbit Jerky in the local market. He had visions of it sitting next to the cash register at thousands of convenience stores and delicatessens nationwide, just like beef jerky products. But Rabbit Jerky wasn't selling so well, he confided.

I could understand why, I told him. People don't want to eat little processed bunnies. In our culture, rabbits are snugly and lovable. Even when they're wise guys. If Warner Bros. ever allowed Elmer Fudd to actually take a bite out of Bugs Bunny, there would be a protest march. But this caller was persistent, as people on a mission usually are.

"There's more rabbit sold than you think," he said.

"Correction," I replied. "Perhaps there's more rabbit sold than we know is being sold."

Indeed, if people are putting rabbit into food, they're . . . well, let's just say they're being very discreet about it. Most American consumers don't want to think they're eating the Easter Bunny.

The caller saw my point, he said.

"That's why I've been thinking of changing the name to *Lapin* Jerky," he said, using the French word for rabbit with an exaggerated accent.

Well, perhaps hasenpfeffer is called hasenpfeffer and not bunny stew for good reason. But you don't find hasenpfeffer on the menus of very many restaurants, and it isn't displayed next to the chopped meat at the supermarket. No matter what you call it, the American masses are not ready for Rabbit Jerky.

Some products will never sell well in the United States because of cultural and societal boundaries that can't be crossed. Let's put it this way: If you're going to skewer a sacred cow, forget about the mass market.

CONCENTRATING TOO MUCH

Because of consumers' concern for the environment, concentrated products have become very popular in recent years. The consequences of despoiling our planet have become a major theme in many school curriculums starting in kindergarten. If parents themselves are not inclined to "recycle, reuse, and conserve," their children are sure to remind them.

One of the most noticeable outcomes of the environmental movement is the trend toward less packaging. Almost overnight, for instance, shrink-wrapped, cardboard CD packages disappeared because of pressure from environmentalists.

Consumers have embraced concentrated products despite some lingering perception problems. Years ago, you had to add water to concentrated cleaners, detergents, fabric softeners, or shampoos to get the necessary consistency. Downy Concentrate, for example, came in a small, environmentally correct bottle. The user poured the contents into the original, big container of Downy, then added water. That's no longer the case, for good reason. People felt gypped when they mixed a small amount of powder or liquid with a whole bunch of H_2O.

Some consumers also believe that once you plop down your money for a packaged product, it should do what it's supposed to do, or taste as good as it's supposed to taste, right out of the box. Who needs the extra work? It's not only the physical act of mixing that's troublesome. Half the time the water splashed or some of the ingredients spilled. Plus, if a mixing bowl was required, it had to be washed.

Hunt's Spaghetti Sauce Maker was a concentrated sauce in a jar with a molded indentation in front that accommodated a packet of herbs and spices. The idea was to add the herbs and spices to suit your own taste. This sounds perfectly reasonable to me because I never use the sauce as it comes. I always add chopped meat or onions or garlic or some spices. But this is one case where I differ from the masses. Most people are loyal to a particular brand of food not only because they like the way it tastes but also because it tastes exactly the same every time they open the package. When people have to mix in the herbs and spices, the taste becomes variable. Or there's a perception that the taste becomes variable.

Spaghetti Sauce Maker also required that water be added—up to two-thirds of a cup depending on the consistency you wanted. This created another degree of variability in addition to reminding the consumer that there's a lot of water in the sauce.

Even though most concentrated products are no longer mixed with water, there's still a psychological barrier among older consumers. People don't want to be reminded of how much water is in the regular products they purchase.

Finally, manufacturers of concentrated products have to contend with one of the great truths of marketing: Consumers often don't read directions or instructions, no matter how clearly you communicate them.

Or they're not sure what the word "concentrated" means. Or deep, deep down they don't believe that a lesser amount of soap powder will really get their underwear as clean as a heaping cupful will. So they use the larger portion. Then they begin to think that they are buying the product too often, and that the manufacturer is just raising its profits by making the package smaller.

By and large, concentrated products are succeeding, but there's still a limit as to how far you can go. As technologically superior as a product may be in the laboratory, it won't sell if people don't believe that they are getting their money's worth. That's what happened with Double Power Wisk.

Wisk was introduced by Lever Brothers in the mid-1950s. It was the first liquid laundry cleanser, at least since the days when women wore bloomers and soap was cooked in farmyard vats. Advertising proclaimed that it was a "miracle" product. Because it was new, consumers gave it a try, but sales eventually dropped. Liquid Wisk cost substantially more than powdered detergents at the time but didn't really get laundry much cleaner.

Then, in the mid-1960s, an advertising man read a research report about troublesome laundry problems. One of those proverbial lightbulbs went off in his head, and the advertising that resulted was worse than a fingernail screeching across a blackboard. Wisk, the American public was informed, could do away with the scourge of "Ring Around the Collar." Wives need no longer feel guilty about sending their husbands into corporate battle with graying shirt collars. The commercials' repetitive whine of "ring around the collar, ring around the collar" seemed just like a schoolyard taunt. The longer the campaign ran, the more grating the commercials seemed to get. Nobody had a kind word to say about them, with one exception. The accountants at Lever Brothers loved the campaign because it made cash registers ring. As annoying as the commercials were, they stuck in consumers' heads and were effective. Sales for Wisk zoomed during the next decade.

Procter & Gamble's first response was liquid Era in 1975, but it didn't really get into the liquid detergent game big time until Tide was liquefied in 1984. As is usually the case when two giants butt heads, the resulting couponing and advertising battle was ferocious. Liquids gained acceptance slowly but surely. In the Northeast, they actually became more popular than powdered detergents; nationwide, about 40 percent of consumers used liquids.

Then, the whole detergent business changed. In 1991, P&G introduced Ultra Powder Tide. Competitors soon unleashed their own ultraconcentrated powders, which proved to be a win-win-win situation. Manufacturing and distribution costs were lower for the manufacturer. Consumers toted a smaller box home and got just as much bang for fewer scoops. Retailers reclaimed some room on their shelves. And, of course, less packaging meant less waste.

P&G launched Ultra Liquid Tide the following year, along with liquid versions of its Cheer, Bold, Solo, and Dash brands. Ultra Liquid Tide came in a 50-ounce bottle that P&G claimed did the same job that its 64-ounce version had done. Lever Brothers lagged behind its global rival but thought it had an ace in the hole. In 1993, it introduced Double Power Wisk, as well as superconcentrated versions of Surf and All. Wisk's 32-ounce bottle—18 ounces less than Tide—purportedly contained all the cleaning power of its 64-ounce regular formula.

Lever Brothers pumped $100 million into advertising and promoting the new product, the largest expenditure ever in the laundry category. It reportedly spent the same amount in research and development costs for Double Power. And while its message reached 98 percent of U.S. homes, it was all for naught. Consumers didn't buy it.

Wisk had crossed a mysterious line. Most shoppers don't read the fine print; many don't even read the big print. Lever was asking shoppers to pay the same amount of money for a package that was half the size of what it used to be. Some continued to pour the same amount of Wisk into their wash—maybe because they didn't read the label, or maybe because they didn't believe it. A half-cup of liquid detergent looks rather feeble against a tub full of kids' dirty clothes, after all. Some of these free-pouring consumers dumped enough Double Power Wisk to produce a sudsy calamity, I've been told. And even if they just poured a little bit more with each load, they still found themselves buying new detergent quicker than they had before. With less liquid to begin with, there was less wriggle room.

There's another reason consumers didn't like the new bottle. They'd become jaded. For years now, manufacturers have put less product into the same size package to maintain retail prices. Everyone knows that coffee, cereal, candy bars, and potato chip packages don't deliver as much product as they once did.

Shoppers simply didn't believe that a package half the size it used to be would deliver just as much punch.

Lever pulled Double Power from the market after about eighteen months of futility. A few months after that, it announced that it would reintroduce Wisk and Surf ultraconcentrates based on the same formulation used by P&G. The Wisk debacle proves, in the end, that it's possible to have too little of a good thing.

D

DESKFAST: A LESSON IN PROFITING FROM CHANGE

You may already have gotten the impression that I'm not happy about a lot of the changes that I've seen in the workplace. That's true, from both a business and a personal perspective. Professionally, I feel that widespread downsizing is resulting in brand managers who are repeating yesterday's mistakes because they and their organizations are totally unaware of the history of their products (see *Alzheimer's, Corporate*). Belt-tightening also has curtailed the noodling-and-doodling time that's so essential to creative people who develop innovative products.

From a personal perspective, it's much more of a dog-eat-dog world out there than it was when I broke into marketing with Colgate-Palmolive some forty years ago. I miss civility. I miss the sense of loyalty people felt to colleagues and their companies. I miss the less harried pace. Jobs, for the most part, were 9 A.M. to 5 P.M. back then. In today's uncertain climate, marketers work ten or twelve hours a day. They're not only afraid they'll lose their own jobs, they're picking up the slack left by those who have already been jettisoned. Many spouses work outside the home because they need to, not because they want to.

As a result of all this work-work-work, families don't eat together except on special occasions. We wind up grabbing meals as we can and gobbling them down while we do something else (whether it's preparing a report that the boss wants in two hours or chilling out with a mindless sitcom on TV). Most of the time, of course, we're eating fast food or its supermarket equivalent because we don't have the time to prepare something "healthy."

Okay, some of you might be saying, tell me something new. I will. But before I do, let me ask you something. If you've noticed all this yourself, why aren't you exploiting these developments? Whether we approve of them or not, they're reality. They are situations begging for solutions, for new products.

For instance, people have long skipped eating breakfast because they don't feel they have enough time to prepare and eat it before they leave home. Given our more frenetic pace, the number of people who eat breakfast at their destination—whether it's work, school, or the gym—has doubled since 1990 according to the NPD Group, a research firm that tracks consumers' eating habits. The phenomenon is becoming so widespread that a word has been coined to describe it: deskfast. Deskrunch and deskdin are sure to follow. They may be murder on the ears, but they're a potential boon to food marketers.

Fast food restaurants such as McDonald's and Burger King have catered to the breakfast-on-the-run crowd for years, of course. But where are you other food marketers?

There's at least one smart manufacturer with its eyes peeled to social trends. Fantastic Foods, which helped to create and popularize the all-natural, instant soup cups category, has introduced instant Hot Cereal Cups. Consumers who want a nutritious meal at their desks simply add hot water to flavors such as Mellow Mango with Oat Bran or Peachberry Wheat and Oats. It's eaten right out of the container. All of the flavors are made with organic whole grains and real fruit and are naturally low in fat and high in fiber. Hot Cereal Cups offer a really healthy alternative to Egg McMuffins and the like, and they take less time to prepare than it takes to detour to a drive-through window.

If I were you, I'd take an inventory of all the developments taking place in society that make you feel that "things aren't what they used to be." When you have established what they are, whether you approve of them or not, take a hard look at whether products in your category have adapted to the change.

There very well may be an opening in the market—as automobile manufacturers discovered during the 1980s baby boomlet—that you can drive a minivan through.

DOING YOUR HOMEWORK

Most marketers aren't trained researchers. They rely on others to conduct research about the prospects for a given product or situation. The best marketers, however, are very good at synthesizing information—combining their knowledge and experience with the results of proprietary research to make best-guess decisions.

Research takes many forms, of course. Demographic data and psychographic musings are available from dozens of firms who provide companies with information about consumer markets. Combined with optimistic spreadsheet projections, these data often paint a very rosy picture that's seldom matched in the real world.

Focus groups are a useful research tool, particularly when several options are being considered, but they have severe limitations. First, focus groups are conducted in extremely contrived conditions. In the real world, people are bombarded by many more choices than they are in a closed room with a rigid set of questions.

Second, the results depend greatly on the ability of the group's moderator. A good moderator stays in the background but has a way of coaxing people's true feelings out of them; bad moderators let groups run away from them entirely. I've seen one strong-willed, vocal participant in a group thoroughly sway the opinions of her peers.

Third, I've found that people often say one thing in public, but act in a totally different way when they're actually shopping in a store. Ask a group of moms if they'd prefer Cereal X, a granola-type grain with nuts and berries, or Cereal Y, a Froot Loops knockoff with twice the sugar. Guess which they'll pick. Guess which will sell better.

Then there are test markets. Test marketing—the sale of a new product in limited or restricted markets—was introduced in the United States some sixty years ago by Procter & Gamble. Today most major companies will introduce products into markets that reflect the demographics of the group they are targeting. Some areas, such as Syracuse, New York, Pittsfield, Massachusetts, and Bakersfield, California, are popular testing grounds because their consumers are a microcosm of the country as a whole.

Testing a product before you throw your full resources behind it is an attractive idea. Theoretically, all of the inherent faults of your concept and of your plan of execution will show up so that you can refine the product and tweak the marketing plan. Your product will be better for the process, and you'll have a better sense about how to approach its distribution and promotion in the national marketplace.

The test market is no sure-fire cure for failure, though. First, there's no substitute for marketing a product in the real world, where promotional efforts and spending meet the competition's response head-on. Second, there are intangibles that are not always apparent in the markets where the products are tested, no matter how precisely they mirror the demographic qualities of target consumers. Finally, competitors occasionally sabotage a test, or sometimes it's inadvertently skewed by competitors' curiosity (see *Falsies*).

If you work for a large corporation, you have many research options available to you, as well as the budget to deploy them. But the real art is in analyzing the data and deciding what's valid and what's not. As Mark Twain observed, there are "lies, damn lies, and statistics." Entrepreneurs, on the other hand, usually have to rely on their own investigations to determine whether or not their dreams are worth pursuing.

I know a young man who came up with an idea of selling branded firewood. He lived in a suburb of a Northeastern city. A wood stove installed in the family room of his home provided supplemental heat on frigid days, as well as a sense of comfort and well-being.

Every year my friend scanned the classified ads to find someone who would sell him decent firewood. He was rarely satisfied with the wood he received from various local woodsmen and garden-supply centers. A supplier who delivered a good mix of wood one year would deliver a batch of logs all cut from the same species of tree the next. Sometimes the wood was too green for safe, efficient burning. Other times he suspected he had been shortchanged on the amount of wood he received. Some years the wood was neatly stacked by the deliverymen; other times it was dumped in a heap that spilled over into his neighbor's yard.

This is just the sort of real-life situation that's fertile territory for new product ideas, and the lightbulb eventually went on in my friend's head. He reasoned that there must be other frustrated homeowners in his community. Why not package a good mix of hard and soft woods as well as kindling in standard sizes and prices? He'd call the product Good Wood, which described the significant attribute of the merchandise in a memorable way. He'd hire courteous drivers to deliver and stack the loads wherever the homeowners wanted. His imagination started to run wild. He envisioned regional sawmills splitting and sawing up logs and shipping them out to satellite distribution centers across the Snowbelt. He thought about selling premium lines, too. Small but pricey bundles of white birch, which would look very elegant sitting in an open hearth between fires, for instance. He even considered importing some peat from Ireland as a specialty item. If you've got an entrepreneurial bone in your body, you no doubt recognize the symptoms of fanaticism.

Before this idea got off the ground, my friend did some basic research. He started by tracking down a couple of families in his village who also owned wood stoves. He discovered that the men salvaged logs from the sides of roads after storms, and actually got a kick out of sawing up and splitting the wood for their wood stoves. That was an inauspicious start. Then he looked up dealers of wood stoves in the Yellow Pages and discovered that there were none within a fifty-mile radius of his home. The reason for this, he discovered when he called the shops, was that most of the homeowners in his area did not share his enthusiasm for hauling logs from a woodpile and keeping a hungry hearth fed. He then called a few chimney sweeps and discovered that although many of his neighbors had open fireplaces where they'd burn logs a few times a year, very few homes in his area actually had wood stoves as he did.

The bottom line, this fellow concluded, was that Good Wood might be a great idea, but certainly not in the area he was considering. There simply were not enough people interested in the product there, and wood chopped and split up into 18- to 24-inch logs was not the easiest product to handle and transport over long distances to other markets.

My friend's research saved him from making a disastrous career change. Instead, he went out and bought a chain saw, ax, and maul. All through the fall, he cuts and splits wood for the next year's wood-burning season. He's got a market of one—himself—but it's a great way to work out tension. And thanks to his research, he's a lot more fortunate than many entrepreneurs who plunge into a business without doing their homework.

DON'T DAWDLE

A doctoral candidate might write a thesis titled "Clairol's Short and Sassy: A Study of an Inflexible Degree of Responsiveness to Environmental Change in the Market." Here's what happened to Short and Sassy shampoo in a nutshell: By the time Clairol launched this product for women with short hair, long hair was becoming popular again. Clairol spent too much time trying to get the formula right.

Similarly, Procter & Gamble took about three years to test a toilet-bowl cleaner called Brigade that slowly released its contents from the tank into the water as you flushed. Meanwhile, the leading toilet-bowl-cleaner companies asked their chemists to knock off the Brigade concept. By the time P&G had fine-tuned Brigade, Vanish and Ty-D-Bol were already well established in the marketplace. (P&G, fed up with having innovative ideas picked off by competitors, has streamlined its test-marketing process since then.)

The timing behind licensed products is particularly crucial. Pepperidge Farm bought the rights to the *Star Wars* name for a line of cookies in the 1980s. By the time the cookies got to market, *Star Wars* had been eclipsed as a hot movie product. (And it was a decade too early for the hoopla generated by the revival of the series in the late 1990s.)

In recent years, marketers have been aligning themselves with movies well before they're released. Sometimes before a final script is written. That's chancy, of course. Potential blockbusters have a nasty habit of turning into plain, old busts. For every successful *Pocahontas*, there's more than one box office bomb. But it's a risk you have to take if you want to play the Hollywood game.

More than ever, victory belongs to the swift. Netscape quickly captured 80 percent of the Internet browser market by flooding it with free copies of its innovative software. Internet software products have a shelf life of about six months. Netscape will lose its advantage overnight if it doesn't stay ahead of its competitors'—particularly Microsoft's—innovations.

Low-tech products must be just as timely. Commemorative hats and T-shirts are on the street within minutes after a team has won a world championship. Kids' fads like Power Rangers and Teenage Mutant Ninja Turtles come and go faster than a SWAT team.

Don't dawdle a day longer than you must, particularly if you are introducing something that you cannot protect through patent or copyright. Get committed early to innovative ideas and move along smartly. Finally, don't look back because, to update baseball great Satchel Paige's quip, something *undoubtedly* will be gaining on you.

DOZEN PRESUMPTIONS GUARANTEED TO HELP YOU FLOP, A

If the very thought of success makes you tremble, if your knees shake at the prospect of launching a product that will put your career into orbit, have I got a solution for you. Twelve of them, in fact. Just fully embrace a few of the presumptions below, cock your eyebrow superciliously, and blithely proceed with your product launch. Before anyone's tempted to promote you to a job that pays too much money and carries too much power, your venture will fall to earth in a blaze of ignominy.

Here, then, are A Dozen Presumptions Guaranteed to Help You Flop:

1. Customers will buy our product because we think it's a good product.

2. Customers will buy our product because it's technologically superior.

3. Customers will immediately perceive that our product is vastly different from all the others on the market.

4. Customers won't feel it's risky to buy from us and cut off their past supplier.

5. Our product will sell itself.

6. Distributors will be desperate to stock our product.

7. Our product will roll out on the precise date we've projected, and we won't spend a penny more than we've budgeted.

8. We will have no problem attracting a talented staff that's as committed to our product's success as we are.

9. We don't have to worry about competitors.

10. Competitors will react to our product predictably, and with dignity and restraint.

11. We'll be able to keep our margins high and will rapidly gain market share.

12. All of the divisions of our company will be behind us 100 percent and their managers will gladly assist us in any way they can.

DOZEN TIPS FOR TRADE SHOWS, A

Trade shows are great for schmoozing and net-working. The food at the banquets isn't all that bad, and the partying (if you're of a certain age) can't be beat. So who cares if you get any exposure for your new product or if you make any sales?

Here, then, are a dozen ways to guarantee that you don't ruin you trade-show experience by processing orders:

1. If you don't have anything new to show this year, trot out something from previous shows. Take the attitude that nobody remembers anything they see at trade shows anyway.

2. Don't bother coming to trade shows with handouts about the products you're introducing. People have great memories.

3. Don't waste space by printing your company name, address, and contact information on every sheet of your material. If trade-show attendees can't effectively organize the literature from hundreds of companies in their giveaway tote bags, they'll never have the presence of mind to call you anyway.

4. If your blow-'em-over presentation doesn't result in an order right there on the show floor, don't worry about following up by phone, fax, or e-mail. You'll get 'em at the next trade show.

5. Be particularly wary about people who leave their business cards, which are printed by the thousands. They are just being polite and you've got a million other things to do.

6. But if telephone follow-up with prospects is un-avoidable, don't bore people with details and facts. When

you look uninformed, it makes other people feel superior. Certainly don't do any homework about whom you are calling when you follow up. People love it when you mistake them for somebody else or assume that they have different responsibilities than they do.

7. If you follow up with a letter or e-mail, send the same information to everybody, ignoring the specific requests you received. Time is money, and individual attention takes time.

8. Ignore phone calls from reporters and editors who would have you believe that they'll give you some free publicity. Ever since Watergate, the media is only interested in running embarrassing exposés.

9. Don't bite if a member of the media asks for samples that he says he wants to photograph. Foil the request by using inferior packaging (padded mailing envelopes are great for this) that will result in the product being rendered totally unphotogenic by the Postal Service or express-delivery service.

10. Better yet, send a different sample than what the editor requested. It's a great way to get rid of old stock. Or send it too late to use. Deadlines should be more flexible than they are.

11. Never deliver what you promise.

12. See #11. Hey, eleven out of twelve is good enough.

E

EXTRANEOUS EXTRAS

People won't buy what they don't want. It's amazing how many of America's most intelligent marketers have forgotten that from time to time, thereby enriching my collection of flops. Jeno Paulucci is one of the forgetful ones.

Paulucci is the marketing genius who started Chun King Chinese food and then made a bundle by selling it off to R.J. Reynolds foods in 1966. After that, he launched a reasonably successful line of frozen pizzas named, with all due self-homage, Jeno's.

One obstacle standing between Jeno and a bigger slice of the home-pizza market, however, was that fabled hero of suburban folklore, the pizza-delivery jockey. And even before Pizza Hut, Domino's Pizza, and Little Caesars were taking home delivery seriously, the local guys were retrofitting the trunks of 1962 Ford Falcons with ovens that kept the cheese warm and the crusts crunchy. People could custom-order a pie and have it at their front door before they had the sodas poured and the paper plates out of the pantry.

Jeno relishes a good battle, and he dreamed up what he thought was the perfect way to compete with pizzeria pizzas. The premium frozen pizza. Jeno packaged his Premium pizza in a heavyweight brown kraft carton similar to what many pizzeria pizzas come in. It was a big pizza. And it tasted good. It was a bit pricey for frozen pizzas at the time—about $6 a pie—but it wasn't out of line with the price of pizzeria pizza. You didn't have to wait thirty minutes for delivery, you could eat it at any time of the day or night, and it was always in your freezer (which never closed for holidays). All you had to do was pop the pie in the oven—a culinary feat even teenage boys are capable of performing. But there was more to this pizza, something that Jeno thought made it the ultimate pie in pizzadom, something that "everyone will want." The pie was packaged with a large number of toppings: packets of olives, peppers, sausage, pepperoni, cheese (of course), onions, and even anchovies. The idea was that consumers could take the frozen pizza home and top it off with precisely the items they wanted, just as they could order them at a pizzeria. And if Mom wanted peppers and Dad wanted just sausage and Missy wanted everything, no problem.

But most people don't want a pie with everything on it. And even allowing for the great variety of tastes within a family, one or more of the packets of ingredients were inevitably dumped into the trash. Consumers who are already paying a higher than usual price for a product are particularly sensitive to throwing away what they paid for. In the end, Paulucci wound up losing a good deal of money on the product, which he promoted heavily. What Paulucci forgot is a fundamental lesson: Consumers will not pay for what they don't want or can't use.

ENVIRONMENT: HOT BUTTON #2 FOR THE MILLENNIUM

The environment has been a hot button for more than a decade, but it's a tricky one to push. Consumers invariably tell pollsters that they'll willingly pay a little more for a product that's friendly to the environment. When they get to the cash register, however, it's usually a different story.

It's also difficult to determine what is actually good for the environment and what is just wishful thinking. In the 1980s, several manufacturers marketed what they believed were biodegradable trash bags. It turned out that the bags did exactly what the manufacturers claimed when they were exposed to sunlight, but would not decompose when they were buried in a landfill, as most of our trash is. The press wrote stories that made it look as if the manufacturers had deliberately misled consumers, which left some marketers wary about trying to do the right thing.

Meanwhile, the debate still rages over whether or not the energy consumed by a service that picks up, washes, dries, and delivers cloth diapers is a greater threat to the environment than disposable diapers. I have even seen articles that suggest that the recycling of aluminum, plastic, and paper is not only economic folly but also has a negligible benefit to the environment.

The popularity of the recycling movement, particularly among young people, does prove one thing: Americans feel that they have a personal stake in preserving the environment for future generations. They feel good when they think they're doing something positive for the ecology or consuming something that's purportedly pure or free of pollutants. They've embraced ultraconcentrated products (up to a limit—see *Concentrating Too Much*) that require less packaging because the water has been taken out. They've embraced boxless deodorants and toothpastes. Consumers recognize the symbol for recycled paper and will use it or buy a product packaged in it, even though it has a slightly duller finish. More cosmetic products appear with the claim "no animal testing," which is becoming an important issue. Organic and natural food products have almost become mainstream.

By all means, sincerely strive to give your product an environmental edge. People want to feel good about what they consume, and marketers want to feel good about what they sell. But also remember that if the product doesn't taste good or isn't handy to use, many of today's consumers will avoid it no matter what claims you can make for its friendliness to the environment.

EXTENSIONS: WHY THEY'RE GOOD

Brand extensions. Line extensions. Product-line extensions. Call them what you will, they have been exploding. According to Marketing Intelligence Service's ProductScan, 63 percent of the products introduced in 1990 in grocery and drugstores were new varieties, formulations, sizes, or packages of existing products, 1 percent were brand extensions, and 36 percent were new brands. Five years later, 77 percent of new products were line extensions, 2 percent were brand extensions, and 21 percent were new brands.

Consumers accept extensions more readily than in the past. Barraged and besieged by new flavors, improved formulas, and handier sizes, their resistance has worn down. And brands that once stood for one big idea now stand for many ideas. In the past, Coca-Cola was a single drink whose formula was considered so precious that only a handful of people knew exactly what it was. Today, Coke is many drinks, many formulas.

In the past, Cadillacs were luxurious, unabashed gas-guzzlers. They appealed to well-to-do consumers who were proud of their wealth. Some of today's Cadillac models would have been considered compact cars during the 1960s and are indistinguishable from less-expensive nameplates. Meanwhile, Japanese automakers who built their reputation by selling tiny, tinny economy cars now manufacture luxury brands such as Lexus and Infiniti that carry as much cachet, if not more, as Cadillac.

In an environment such as this, it's possible that anything might stick. Okay, maybe the public wasn't ready for Jack Daniel's Nature-Glo charcoal briquettes or Häagen-Dazs liqueur. But no one would have guessed a generation ago that a trade name like Calvin Klein (or just the initials CK) would successfully brand such diverse products as fragrances, blue jeans, and underwear. Or that Sony would produce the action-filled motion picture that you watch on your Sony TV and VCR.

Here's why line extensions are so popular among marketers today:

• *It's cheaper to introduce an extension.* Both the trade and consumers are familiar with the brand and its attributes. Snapple would be crazy to mint a new brand every time it added a flavor. A pasta maker would be nuts to slap one label on its angel hair and a different one on its fettuccine.

• *An extension can expand the brand's franchise.* As popular as Cheerios are, some kids won't touch the stuff because it doesn't contains gobs of sugar like most other kids' cereals. So General Mills widened the brand's appeal by introducing Honey Nut Cheerios. Health-conscious moms who trust the Cheerios name bought into the extension because the cereal contained such wholesome ingredients as honey and nuts. Egged on by that success, the company brought out Frosted Cheerios. It, in turn, is reportedly doing better than any new cereal product has ever done.

• *An extension is a way to determine, quickly and cheaply, if a fad is going to be a trend or just a fad.* Suppose trendsetters say that mauve will be the hot new color. Perhaps. One easy way to find out is to make mauve another color selection in your line of facial tissue to see how well it sells.

• *An extension is a way to control shelf space.* It's as simple as this: If you occupy a space, your competitor doesn't. This reasoning is misguided, however, because it often supports the needs of the organization over those of the consumer. But to realize how effective this technique can be, I always envision a red-and-white wall of Campbell's soup cans.

• *An extension is an implied guarantee of consistency.* This reason gets to the soul of brand marketing. Consumers choose a particular brand not only because they like it but because they know that they'll be getting the same quality, time after time. With the glut of choices in the supermarket, consumers see a familiar label as a beacon in stormy seas.

The Walt Disney Company has slapped the Disney name on everything from magazines to retail stores to television channels in recent years. Consumers expect that those products will offer appropriate fare for everyone in the family. When Disney produces more risqué entertainment, it uses a different brand name, such as Touchstone Pictures. Its hockey team, the Mighty Ducks of Anaheim, has a wholesome image even though hockey is a very rough sport.

• *If an extension doesn't move, you can quickly make a substitution.* If taupe has replaced mauve as the hot color at the spring fashion shows, you simply cease production of mauve facial tissue with little harm to your basic white, pink, yellow, and green lines.

• *An extension can revive a flagging brand.* Hershey's Kisses were for fuddy-duddies, candy you gave out at Halloween because you got them yourself when you were a kid. Hershey's Hugs—Kisses with a nut inside—seem to have revived the whole brand. Recently, I saw them served right next to the Brie at a chichi reception.

• *An extension can scare off competition.* There's no quicker way to discourage competitors than to glom on to a hot idea by slapping the label of an established brand on the package. Martinson's Microwaveable Coffee Bags, for example, was an innovative product that developed a following in the Northeast. Martinson's all but disappeared after Folgers and Maxwell House, the two top-selling coffee brands, copied the concept.

EXTENSIONS: WHY THEY'RE BAD

Extensions are the lazy man's way to jump-start sales.

"Now just hold on a minute," I can hear you yelling. "You just gave me eight great reasons why extensions are good."

I did indeed. But I'm not at all sure I accept many of them. In essence, they are rationalizations that I've heard over the years. They are conventional wisdom, handed down from upper-level managers to middle managers, and then back up the line.

More often than not, I believe that an extension satisfies the internal needs of marketers rather than the needs of their customers. Product-line extensions are particularly seductive but lethal. I don't think consumers will be excited by the Betty Crocker line of cereal any more than their fancy was tickled by Kellogg's 4 Minute Fudge (see *Besmirching Your Good Name*). Sure, those venerable brand names demand attention and goose initial sales. But in the end, Betty Crocker means baked goods and Kellogg's means cereal.

Here are some reasons why line extensions should not be as popular as they are:

• *When there are too many extensions, the brand becomes blurred.* Consumers go to Burger King for burgers; they go to Pizza Hut for pizza. Burger King pizza and Pizza Hut burgers cloud the issue. People wonder if something has gone wrong with the core products. To keep customers coming back, you should do what you do best, only better.

• *An extension cannibalizes sales.* Lysol Deodorizing Cleaner is a general-purpose cleanser that can be used anywhere in the house. Consumers naturally buy less of it if they are attracted to Lysol's extensions for particular areas of the house, such as Lysol Antibacterial Kitchen Cleaner or Lysol Disinfectant Bathroom Cleaner for Basin, Tub, Tile.

Extensions that drastically improve the effectiveness of a product can be particularly nettling. For generations, servants polished the silver of the English upper class every week using Goddard's Plate Polish, later renamed Silver Polish. When Goddard developed a brand extension that prolonged the shine for months, I advised the company to double the retail price instead of raising the price by pennies, as it was planning. The improved polish would be used perhaps a fifth as often as the old standard. (To boost sales, I told Goddard to use the extra money to advertise the new product far and wide.)

• *An extension divides the existing pie into smaller slices.* A new flavor or package size usually does not draw customers to the product segment. At best, it converts customers from other brands. Customers for Ice beer—

whether it's Budweiser's or Molson's—aren't coming from the ranks of wine drinkers.

• *An extension may make sales surge while hiding fundamental weaknesses in the product.* Slap a popular brand name on any product and consumers will try it. But unless it serves a real need, sales will shrivel as soon as the novelty wears off. Pepsi A.M. was a breakfast cola. People in test markets were willing to wake up to it. Once.

• *An extension usually addresses the wants and needs of the marketer or of a brand manager rather than those of the consumer.* It's less risky to extend a successful product than to create an entirely new brand. There's less internal resistance. Less capital to invest. And who cares if it flops? In today's corporate environment, what brand manager knows where he or she will be working after the next quarter?

• *Extensions can undermine brand loyalty.* As I write, the Miller Brewing Company is again attempting to revive its namesake beer, plain old Miller. Miller Lite all but killed Miller. But Miller Lite, positioned and advertised as cleverly as it was, would have been just as successful if it had been called Candlestick-Maker Lite.

• *Extensions can cost you customers.* Healthy Choice frozen meals were so phenomenally successful that ConAgra couldn't resist slapping the label on a variety of other packaged foods, from soups to cereals. The line grew very quickly, but quality was uneven. If a potential customer tastes the so-so soup first and hates it, he will never try its superior frozen entrées.

ETHNICITY: HOT BUTTON #3 FOR THE MILLENNIUM

Until recently, the typical American meal was as bland as the northern European cuisine that was its inspiration. But Americans have begun to enjoy hotter and spicier foods. And the more we eat, the more we want. These products have become such big business that there are several specialty trade shows devoted solely to spicy foods.

Why have our tastes changed so radically?

First, there have been greater numbers of Latinos and Asians among recent immigrants, and their foods are spicier than most British, Irish, German, or even Italian, cuisine. Mexican, Chinese, Japanese, and Thai foods also continue on an upswing in popularity.

Second, health activists made us aware of the hazards of consuming too much sodium. As a response, salt was reduced in many brands. Less salt means less taste. To compensate, manufacturers have added other flavoring. For example, is there a spice that hasn't been added to your favorite brand of potato chips?

Ethnic fads, such as Cajun or Tex-Mex cooking, will continue to pop up. And when they subside, they'll leave a whole new body of recipes—and taste sensations and expectations—in their wake.

One trend to look out for is Eastern European cuisine. Two retail stores in my small community already specialize in Russian food. Even though Ithaca's a college town, which makes it an excellent place to spot trends-in-the-making, there aren't that many students of Russian descent here.

A good place to spot future cooking trends is the annual immigration figures issued by the government. A popular metaphor used to be that America was a "melting pot." The idea was that the cultures of various countries would all blend together. A more appropriate metaphor today might be "salad bowl." We're all mixed together, but each ingredient retains its distinctive, individual taste.

F

FOOLING WITH YOUR CASH COW

It took Pepsi-Cola, the soft drink, the better part of a century to seriously compete with Coca-Cola. When I was a youngster, in fact, the only reason to buy a Pepsi was because it promised "twice as much" fluid for the same price (which was, would you believe, five cents for twelve ounces?). Now, Pepsi is generally perceived as hip, and Coke as stodgy, even though it still ranks as the number two soft drink in overall sales.

PepsiCo, the company, also has come a long way since chairman Donald Kendall induced Nikita Khrushchev, the Soviet leader, to guzzle a Pepsi for the cameras during the height of the Cold War. That one swig instantaneously turned PepsiCo into a global power. It has expanded shrewdly since then, both geographically and strategically. In fact, when you add together the revenue from divisions such as Frito-Lay, Pizza Hut, Taco Bell, and KFC, PepsiCo's annual sales are about double those of the Coca-Cola Company (although it announced in January 1997 that it wanted to spin off its restaurants to its shareholders, forming an independent, publicly traded company).

Why then has PepsiCo been acting lately as if it's on a suicide mission? Is there an organizational Fear of

Success? Or is there something in the sugar-flavored water at company headquarters that causes a corporate compulsion to fool with its cash cows?

Every time I go into a Pizza Hut, for example, they seem to be pushing a new product. Often it has nothing to do with pizza. Every advertisement seems to make a new promise. I don't know what Pizza Hut really stands for anymore.

Yes, it behooves the market leader in pizza to offer innovations in pizza. Pizzas with cheese-stuffed crusts have been a big hit. But dozens of other products have come and gone in recent years. Some of them I've liked—such as a crust stuffed with spices—but they've disappeared. Others were ridiculous by any standard. Why would I want to buy cut-rate chicken wings at a Pizza Hut? Bread sticks did not enhance the Pizza Hut brand name one iota either. And what was that "outer-space miracle," Boli "pocket" pizza, all about? It was ahead of its time as a concept—pocket food is the rage right now—but positioning it as a "gift from outer space" was just plain stupid. People can relate to trying a tasty new meal from Italy; Pluto is not known for its fine cuisine.

Pizza Hut reminds me of a boxer throwing wild punches in the hope that one of them will land. One of its ad campaigns in recent years asked the question "Did you enjoy our stuff?" My immediate reaction was "What stuff?" I didn't think Pizza Hut sincerely cared about me, or anyone else, because even if I did like its stuff, chances are they'd be pushing different stuff the next time I visited. That shouldn't be. I should know exactly what Pizza Hut offers, what it stands for. If a product is worth introducing, it needs more than a month or two to make an impact. You build brand loyalty by giving customers a reason to be loyal. When you're inconsistent, you're Fooling with Your Cash Cow.

Pepsi's introduction of Crystal Pepsi in 1992 was even more baffling. It's the quintessential example of

Fooling with Your Cash Cow by slapping a priceless name on the label of a new product to goose short-term sales. The company could have undermined all the goodwill that the Pepsi brand name has accumulated over many years. Here's how it happened.

By the early 1990s, a new niche was developing in the beverage business, but it was difficult to say exactly what it was. Brands such as Snapple, which was "made of the best stuff on earth," Sundance, Original New York Seltzer, and Clearly Canadian racked up sales among young people with retail prices that made Coke and Pepsi executives drool. The beverages were dubbed "New Age." They were "natural," "light," "holistic," "clear," "effervescent"—whatever those terms meant. In fact, the category was as amorphous as New Age music, which, lullingly sweet as it may be, is unmemorable and 100 percent unhummable. But because New Age had become a $2.5 billion market by 1992, PepsiCo felt that it had a divine right to a piece of the action.

At the time, Clearly Canadian, without a shred of costly mass-market advertising, had become the best-selling brand in the sweetened sparkling water segment of the category. It packed about the same amount of calories per serving as a regular Coke or Pepsi did, but its blue-tinged, elegantly shaped bottle had an understated look that made you think otherwise. It looked as unadulterated as rainwater. It was the kind of bottle that a yuppie could proudly take to his health club. It wasn't some laid-back brand from the hinterlands, however, content to capture a niche market.

"Our whole mandate is to replace any other beverage

the human body may be consuming," declared Clearly Canadian president Douglas L. Mason. "Milk is as much a competitor as Coca-Cola."*

Those were fighting words, and the challenge did not go unnoticed by Pepsi. It forged an alliance with Lipton to attack the Snapple segment of the market by distributing ready-to-drink iced teas, an arrangement that has proven very lucrative over the years. It made a similar deal with Ocean Spray to distribute such juice drinks as Cranapple, Cran-Grape, Cran-Raspberry, Cran-Strawberry, and Crantastic. Pepsi's big plans, however, were for a new drink it developed on its own. It had the same basic flavor that Americans adore: cola. What it did not have were caffeine, preservatives, artificial flavoring, and—most important of all—color. It was clear.

Let's put this into perspective.

The period from about the time the presidential election campaign of 1992 was gathering momentum to somewhere in 1993 was, in fact, the Year of the Clear Product. That presidential campaign was all about "change," you may recall, and the cry for "reinventing government" had propelled Democrat Bill Clinton into the White House. Pundits will tell you that the lack of substantive change under his leadership is what also brought about the "Republican Revolution" of 1994. Whatever political stripe we wore, we wanted a return to what we perceived as simple, basic values. To purity. To naturalness. To unadulterated straight talk. To honesty.

*Quoted in "Water? No! 'New Age' Soda? Clearly," *The New York Times*, January 4, 1992.

Whether it had anything to do with our desire for pure politics or not, the market was besieged by a number of other "clear" products. Ivory Soap Liquid, Palmolive for Sensitive Skin dishwashing detergent, Tab Clear soda, China Cola Clear, Close Up Crystal toothpaste, Clear Choice mouthwash, Crystal Fresh Lavoris mouthwash, and Miller Clear beer, for example. Windex, which long ago established that window cleaners should be a particular tint of blue, introduced a clear all-purpose cleaner. There were clear deodorants, clear antiperspirants, clear cosmetics. Amoco brought out a clear gasoline; Coors launched Zima Clearmalt beverage. Things got so out of hand that *Saturday Night Live* created a parody commercial featuring "Crystal Gravy." It was "lighter, cleaner, more transparent." Even the lumps were invisible.

Clear products are nothing new, of course. Clarity has represented purity at least since the late nineteenth century, when Pears, the transparent soap from Britain, was widely advertised as "a specialty for improving the complexion." More recently, and more relevant, 7-Up's sales surged when it launched its "uncola" ad campaign in the 1970s. I vividly remember the actor Geoffrey Holder, dressed in a white suit and fedora, talking about the "uncola nut" with a lilting Caribbean accent. I also remember how refreshing and pure the carbonated liquid looked as it poured out of a bottle, which was beaded with drops of moisture.

"Ahhhhhhhhhhhhhh," Holder said as he took a sip. I felt as if my own thirst was quenched.

The point is that Pepsi was smart to pay attention to the growing New Age market. It was also clever to develop a clear drink, which immediately telegraphed a purity message. But why in the world give the drink a cola taste? And why in the name of all that is valuable in a brand name call it Crystal *Pepsi*?

Consumers buy a product because they can make basic assumptions about it, having been conditioned by years and years of consumption and advertising. Pepsi is cola. Pepsi is sweet. Pepsi is refreshing. Pepsi is good. Pepsi is a soft drink. Pepsi is brown—even if it has its sugar or caffeine removed. Crystal Pepsi was something else.

One early commercial positioned Crystal Pepsi against bottled waters. The ad showed a group of Frenchmen—obviously Perrier devotees—sitting at a table overlooking a countryside of grass and trees. The people at the table were discussing a new beverage that one of them had sampled. He raved about it. It was bottled, it was clear, and so on. For each attribute, someone replied, "But so is ours." Then the man mentioned that the new drink had a pleasant taste. The others emitted a simultaneous "Ohhhhhh." But they were perhaps the only people on earth who accepted Crystal Pepsi as a New Age beverage that tasted good. No one I spoke to, including a couple of hundred college students who were Pepsi's target market, thought it was anything other than just another cola. And not a very tasty one at that.

Suppose, however, that consumers not only liked the taste of Crystal Pepsi but also believed all the hype about this clear version of the brand that they had been drinking since they were kids. Pepsi was telling them that absolutely none of the qualities that drew them to the brand in the first place had any abiding value. The brown coloring was gone because it was not natural. There were no preservatives, which suggested that the ones in regular Pepsi were not healthy. Ditto for caffeine. There was a cola taste, but it was distinctly different from the taste they'd always loved.

Admittedly, most consumers didn't ponder these issues. Consumers generally are quite decisive. They hear an advertisement or see a store display and quickly decide whether or not to give a new product a try. That posed another danger.

Consumers who never drank a New Age beverage before and were attracted to Crystal Pepsi might be tempted to buy competitive products just to see how they compared. And they might very well have decided that those brands were better and turned into New Age beverage consumers at the expense of brown soda.

PepsiCo seems to be wantonly experimenting with its flagship brand. For several summers, the company produced a succession of strange fruit-flavored versions of Pepsi Cola that were only available for a few months. Whether or not you liked these flavors, they were gone as soon as autumn rolled around. What purpose did that serve? Consumers who wanted the flavors and couldn't get them felt abandoned; consumers who didn't like them felt betrayed.

Pepsi should thank its lucky stars that Crystal Pepsi was a stinker. It's one thing to lose money (in this case, reportedly about $100 million in development and advertising costs) on a poor product. It's quite another to produce a product that's so good it undercuts the positioning of your main brand. If you succeed in making the consumer think that qualities they strongly associate with a brand have no value, they will doubt the value of the product itself.

FIGHT FROM A POSITION OF STRENGTH

Nothing can stop competitors from trying to knock off your new-product success with me-too products. But if you find some high ground from which to fight the battle, you'll be tough to overtake.

Nabisco seized the high ground with its Teddy Grahams cookies, which came on the market in 1988 and immediately had annual retail sales of more than $150 million. Although the new cookie was an overnight success, it was the result of about three years of careful, secretive planning and development. Indeed, Nabisco took ideas that were nearly a century old and made them fresh in a way that could not be duplicated by other marketers.

Teddy Grahams were a novel recombination of two of Nabisco's longtime winners, Graham Crackers and

Barnum's Animal Crackers. The graham cracker has a good-for-you aura that dates from its origins as a health food created by a nineteenth-century minister, Sylvester Graham. Mothers have long given graham crackers and milk to their kids as a "healthy" after-school snack.

Animal Crackers have been part of Nabisco's lineup since 1902, when it attached the name of the famous showman P. T. Barnum to a cookie that many bakers had been making for decades. There are sixteen creatures in Nabisco's Animal Crackers menagerie, including a lion, tiger, hyena, rhino, standing bear, and sitting bear.

There's good reason why only the bear is depicted twice—the same reason Nabisco chose a teddy bear as the model for its bite-size cookies aimed at young kids (as eaters) and their parents (as buyers). Everybody thinks of teddy bears as being warm and cuddly. They represent security and continuity. Adults remember their childhood favorites with longing and still buy them today. For example, a Vermont company promotes teddy bears dressed up in different costumes as an alternative to sending flowers. Some collectible teddy bears are far too expensive to give to children for play, but they have universal appeal because they speak to the child in all of us.

The name Teddy Grahams was itself a significant point of difference between the new product and existing cookies, not to mention the parade of me-too products that quickly followed it to market. Bold packaging, excellent in-store merchandising, and strong advertising support also played a major role in Teddy

Grahams' success, as did the popular honey, cinnamon, and chocolate flavors. But the combination of the playful-sounding "Teddy" with the wholesome-sounding "Grahams" was a preemptive stroke of genius.

Dozens of me-too brands hit the market within a few months of the Teddy Grahams launch. Sunshine came out with QT Bears Oatmeal Cookies. Sun Valley introduced Munchee Bears Honey Graham Cookies. Other products included: Tasty Cake Bakery Fresh Tasty Bears Honey Graham Cookies, Keebler Baby Bear Cookies with fudge frosting, and a Limited Edition of Honey Graham Bears Graham Snacks in a coin bank container from Street Kids.

The names of these me-too brands, which all tried to combine bear imagery with a healthy message, were torturous to pronounce. Teddy Grahams says it all, simply and distinctly. It has a built-in recognition factor with no negatives attached to it. Other manufacturers really could not duplicate Nabisco's effort, no matter how tasty their cookies might have been.

FUN: HOT BUTTON #4 FOR THE MILLENNIUM

I've read that you use fewer muscles when you laugh than you do when you frown. I don't know what that means, necessarily, but I do know that people like food that makes them laugh—in the appropriate setting, of course. I wouldn't try to get cute with a new brand of caviar. But food that's fun to prepare, pronounce, or eat has something special going for it. Always has.

Remember how exciting it was to pop popcorn in

a covered pot on top of the stove? Can't you just hear the *ping ping ping ping ping ping pingpingpingpingping* sound that the kernels made as they bounced off the inside of the lid? And then the whole tempo slowed down again. It always seemed like magic when I uncovered the lid to find a pot filled with steaming, exploded kernels.

Have you ever used your spoon to capture the undissolved morsels of Nestle Quik floating in a glass of milk?

Did you ever crumble your cookies in your ice cream when you were a kid? It was the only way you'd have eaten that crunchy combination before the mid-eighties because cookies and cream weren't packaged together as a best-selling, lip-smacking dessert before then.

Ice cream has been a particularly fun category in recent years. I get a kick just reading the latest funny names. Ben & Jerry, Vermont's counterculture entrepreneurs who invented Cookies and Cream, did it first with flavors like Cherry Garcia, but now even upscale mainstream brands such as Häagen-Dazs inject humor into their names. And why not? Ice cream, after all, is not a gourmet meal (except in tony French restaurants, where even the salt is gourmet).

I should point out that cereals don't have to be as serious as Meuslix to make it in the health-conscious 1990s. The spirit that created Froot Loops and Cocoa Puffs is alive and well. Dunk-A-Balls under the Wheaties brand is proof of that, although I think that General Mills went too far with it. The idea was for children to play tabletop basketball by shooting small bits of cereal through a hoop that they cut out of the back of the cereal box. You'll never see me write that parents like to see their kids have fun *playing* with their food. Any product that encourages food follies is taking on a huge challenge—unless it's a product that can be purchased directly by kids.

There's always a bunch of new confectionery items on the market—from tubes of bubble gum to small plastic packages that look like cellular phones—that will have a short but financially sweet life as humorous novelty items. How about Cotton Candy Bubble Gum? Or lollipops the colors of Dennis Rodman's hair? You're laughing, right? Kids bought them. Nobody ever went broke pandering to the sensibilities of ten year olds, as long as the product was priced right and distributed correctly.

FIRE IN THE BELLY

Suzanne Hilou, an accountant by training, was a stockbroker by profession. She hated it. Her own mother describes her as the type of person who "would do anything not to have a real job." Suzanne found her deliverance from "real" work by becoming the founder, product-developer, marketer, salesperson, conceptualizer, market researcher, and chief hunch player for a company she calls Taste Teasers.

Hilou has the fire in the belly that has been apparent in every successful (not to mention quite a few unsuccessful) entrepreneur I've ever met. In her case, though, I mean that literally as well as figuratively.

Hilou started making and selling pepper jelly in 1992. She enjoyed modest success selling it around her Dallas home. Pepper jelly, for all you Yankees, is a versatile hot condiment that's mixed with cream cheese and spread on crackers, used as a dip, or thrown into any number of recipes that need a little spicing up. It's great, too, with a forkful of ham, lamb, or roast beef.

One day, Hilou got the wacky idea of mixing the jalapeño-based flavor of her jelly with another delicious taste, chocolate. She figured chocolate-filled spicy candies might be a cute novelty, a gimmick that would appeal to Texans who take great pride in their fireproof palates. She came up with a good name (Hot Chocolates), a clever tag line ("Fine Chocolate that Bites Back"), and an attractive black box with a bright red-pepper logo on the front. Then she went knocking on Neiman Marcus's door.

There are plenty of stories about prescient store buyers who saw something in a product that no one else did and placed an order that launched a home-based enterprise on the road to fame and fortune. This is not one of them. The Neiman Marcus buyer thought the box looked tacky and said she hated jalapeño.

But Hilou was not about to let this setback distract her from her twenty-four-hour-a-day mission to avoid regular work. She toted Hot Chocolates to a New York show run by the National Association for the Specialty Food Trade in the fall of 1993. The product was a hit with buyers from a variety of locales. The response surprised even Hilou. The package that was deemed unsuitable for Neiman Marcus is now exported to some of the finest department stores in London. And the candy is no gimmick in Japan, where hot flavors are very popular. Buyers from across the U.S. have also placed orders.

Hilou quickly added White Chocolate and Chocolate with Peanut Butter to the Taste Teasers line. Then she launched two sauces, Jalapeño Hot Fudge Sauce and Jalapeño Hot Fudge Peanut Butter, in wide-mouthed jars. Then she developed Jalapeño Chocolate Pecans and Jalapeño Chocolate Almonds.

I don't think that Nestlé is worried that Taste Teasers will usurp its position in the global chocolate market. Nor is Hilou's success keeping marketers in Hershey, Pennsylvania, awake at night. And Taste Teasers has yet to break into Neiman Marcus. But because she had a fire in the belly, Hilou is making a living doing something that she loves to do—and for some people that's exactly as big as a market needs to be.

FALSIES

Some things are not as robust as they appear to be on the surface. For instance, why would a new product sell out in a test market but flop when it goes national?

I see a lot of hands waving out there. How about you?

Hmmmm. That's true. Shoppers often buy on trial but decide the product stinks. Bad news travels fast among consumers. But that's not the answer I'm looking for today.

Okay, I admit it's a trick question. But listen up, because this is something you won't find in your textbook. I've learned it by trial and error. Literally.

I've often purchased samples on behalf of clients. As a result, I've screwed up the results of more than one market test.

Many years ago, for example, a shampoo called Wash & Comb hit test markets. It promised to eliminate tangles. Competitors were extremely interested and bought thousands of samples. My consulting firm alone purchased 3,000 bottles in the Atlanta market. As a result, Wash & Comb looked like a sure winner. But real people weren't buying it; other marketers were. It bombed when it rolled out nationally.

I resolved then and there to notify a company whenever I bought an inordinate amount of product, and I do. But some executives prefer to keep their heads in the sand.

Hunt Wesson, which owned popcorn market-leader Orville Reddenbacher, hired my firm to buy samples of Cracker Jack Extra Fresh Popping Corn when it was tested in a market near me. First, we cleaned out the store shelves. Then we went directly to the Grand Union warehouse to purchase by the case. Time after time. All told, we sent hundreds of cases to Hunt Wesson. A Grand Union executive told us that we were just about the only people buying the product.

I knew I'd destroyed the test. I left messages for both the brand manager at Borden, which owned Cracker Jack, and its ad agency. I said that I had been the major purchaser. Neither called back for details. Bad news doesn't travel well among executives who might wind up with egg on their faces.

The product flopped when it was taken national.

Most competitors aren't as willing to spread bad news as I am, so make sure your test products are really being bought and used by consumers, not analyzed and reverse-engineered by rivals.

FAILURE IS OPPORTUNITY

Some 2,500 years ago, the Chinese philosopher Lao-tzu observed that "failure is an opportunity."

Those who succeed are not afraid to take a risk to pursue a goal or dream. That means they aren't afraid to fail. And when they do fail, they're willing to take another risk. They persist.

Irene Waters and her husband, Peter, refinanced their house on a hunch that she could re-create and successfully market a spun-sugar candy she fondly remembered eating as a girl in upstate New York. On very special occasions, Irene's father would bring home a glass jar of candy sticks made of a thin, satin-silver sugar shell that shimmered in the light. They were filled with chocolate and nuts. As she watched her own children around holiday times, Irene would remember the treat and wonder why it was no longer available.

The reason, she learned after much research, was that candy making had become a mass-market industry and the spun-sugar candy she relished eating as a child was "difficult" and "time-consuming" to make properly. That didn't deter Waters.

In a dusty warehouse she located a rundown machine that could produce the candy and had it restored. Further research turned up an elderly gentleman who knew how to run the machine and spin the candy. It was no easy task. The expert told Waters that even after twenty years of experience, candy makers still had difficulty making pulled hard candy. She soon learned how difficult "difficult" could be. Having thrown her family's life savings and the $40,000 proceeds of

the house refinancing into her new business, Waters missed the crucial Christmas season in her first year, 1986, because she decided not to sell any candy until she could make it well with consistency.

"I threw away thirty thousand pieces of candy weighing thousands of pounds as I worked on perfecting the recipe," Waters says.

The fact that Hearts and Flowers Candy Company is thriving more than a decade later, with a wide assortment of confections sold in a variety of channels, is testimony to the power of trial and error. In the beginning, Waters suffered defeat after defeat. But once she discerned what she was doing wrong, her victories began to outnumber her defeats. And Waters realized that failure was a necessary ingredient in the recipe for success.

"There are no secrets to success," Colin Powell once said. "It is the result of preparation, hard work, learning from failure."

That's what staying in business is all about. Learning from your losses. Persisting. Knowing that failure always presents new opportunities. Yes, it sounds old-fashioned. Ideas that endure for 2,500 years usually do.

FUTURISTS BEARING PROGNOSTICATIONS

Beware of them.

If I were starting out as a new-product consultant today, maybe I'd bill myself as a "Futurist" along with everybody else.

Futurists don't need a heck of a lot of hands-on experience to gaze into the next decade. And they don't need to be right, either.

All you need to be a successful Futurist is a clever hypothesis that's not too different from what people already suspect, a firm voice, and a convincing presentation. And, of course, a platform to spout from—but there seems to be no end to the conferences and trade shows that need entertainers.

The real trick is to be just a tad ahead of your audience. Reinforce the ideas they already have, while suggesting you've got an inside track on the information that's driving other marketers' decisions. (That's how to ring up the big bucks with private consultations.)

It doesn't hurt to have an outrageous prediction, sprinkled with carefully placed ifs, probablys, and maybes. Your forecast will be completely forgotten by 99.9 percent of the audience by the time it doesn't come true. Those ifs, probablys, and maybes will square you with the other 0.1 percent. Besides, Futurists can bank on most people retiring before their prognostications come due.

I doubt that many people remember the musings

of a Futurist who predicted twenty years ago that we'd be driving our cars through tunnel-like, shelf-lined supermarkets to pick out the goods we wanted. I'm sure he'd like to forget it himself.

Or how about all those Futurists who predicted that we'd be bored stiff by too much leisure time? They are probably—notice my waffle—earning top dollar making fresh projections even as I write.

Talk about renewable resources. There's nothing as resilient as blarney.

G

GO WITH THE FLOW

Your consumers may not be who you expected them to be when you were designing your product.

Kimberly-Clark originally advertised Kleenex as a cold-cream remover. Sales were poor. When it discovered that people were using Kleenex as a disposable handkerchief, it wisely switched its advertising message to support nose blowing. Kleenex suddenly became a hot product. Most homes in the United States today have several boxes of tissues open in different rooms—far broader usage than the product would have gotten as a cold-cream remover.

You never really know how big a market may become. No one in 1993 was predicting that the Internet would become as popular as it did just two years later. Who could have thought in the 1950s, when automobiles were huge and heavily stylized, that the tiny, homely Volkswagen Beetle would become a popular automobile in the 1960s, paving the way for a wave of fuel-efficient Japanese imports in the 1970s? Certainly not some otherwise-astute businessmen in Detroit. And, in a classic business-school case history, IBM failed to see the potential for the personal computer until the 1980s. Indeed, who would have thought that fifty years after IBM showed off its prototype main-frame computer Eniac, 34 percent of American house-holds would have PCs that were a fraction of its size (Eniac weighed thirty tons and contained 18,000 vacuum tubes) and yet could outperform it a thousand-fold? In fact, IBM's fabled chairman Thomas Watson once said, "I think there is a world market for maybe five computers."

Sometimes your market defines itself.

I recently heard a story about the origins of fabric softeners that illustrates how a simple idea can be parlayed into a big business.

Before the 1960s, disposable diapers did not exist. Mothers used a cleaning service or washed the diapers at home. The diapers were often rigid when they came out of the dryer, particularly after repeated washings. This chafed the baby's skin. So Procter & Gamble tried to develop a product that would make the laundered diapers, as well as baby's other clothes, softer. The result was Liquid Downy, the first successful fabric softener. P&G rolled it out in 1961. (That same year it also introduced the first disposable diaper, Pampers.)

Liquid Downy was poured directly into the washing machine. Over the years, fabric softeners have evolved. First they were aerosol sprays used in the dryer, then they were incorporated into sheets that also went into the dryer. Later, they were added to the laundry detergents. Many people double up, using a softener-fortified detergent in the washing machine and a softener sheet (which also eliminates "static cling") in their dryers. But the biggest change has not been technological advances. It has been the expansion of the market.

A product that P&G developed to make babies—and their moms—happy has enjoyed much wider usage. Fabric softeners have been as big a boon to kids and adults as they were to babies. Underwear no longer feels like sackcloth, jeans and shirts aren't stiff as boards, sheets and towels don't scratch like sandpaper. Not incidentally, by the time that disposable diapers replaced cloth on most of America's changing tables, P&G had extended the franchise of fabric softeners to include clothing for the whole family.

The lesson of fabric softeners is that you can't always predict whom your consumers will be in the long run. Similarly, Breathe Right nasal strips, which are butterfly-shaped bandages placed on the bridge of the nose, were designed to help snorers sleep better. But then athletes such as the all-pro wide receiver Jerry Rice started to wear them because they felt the product improved the flow of oxygen to their lungs during games.

Although the marketer, CNS, made no claims that wearing the strip improved athletic performance, sales took off when Rice and other players generated free publicity prior to the January 1995 Super Bowl. Drugstores posted hand-lettered signs that said, BREATHE RIGHT IN STOCK. Stroll down to a Pop Warner football game today, and you'll see fifty-pounders wearing Breathe Right just like their heroes. Breathe Right sales for the third quarter of 1994, prior to its national exposure, were less than $700,000. A year later, they were more than $10 million.

Your product—or a competitor's—may have a wider or different appeal than you anticipated. Be on the lookout for unexpected uses, and go with the flow.

GREASY, GLOPPY, AND GLORIOUS

When people go out for a fast-food meal, they know exactly what they are getting: a usually fatty, frequently greasy, often salty, and extremely tasty cure for a rumbling stomach.

"Healthy fast food" makes about as much sense as no-risk rock climbing. No danger, no thrill. No fat, no taste (see *Proof of the Pudding Is in the Eating, The*).

In 1991, McDonald's launched McLean Deluxe, a "healthy" hamburger. It essentially was a response to consumer groups and nutritionists who were ranting about the amount of fat and cholesterol in fast foods. Many other fast-food chains also responded to the critics by developing a, shall we say, *less unhealthy* meal of one kind or another.

McLean Deluxe contained a seaweed derivative that replaced animal fat to bond the beef together. By the time McDonald's killed it five years after its debut, McLean Deluxe had come to symbolize all of the "healthy" fast-food alternatives. It tasted awful and sold poorly.

Right after it came to market, a marketing executive familiar with its development told me that it really didn't matter if it sold well or not. McDonald's was reaping a lot of positive public relations, he said, by offering healthier food.

If that was the case, it was very expensive PR.

McDonald's reportedly invested $25 million to $50 million in the seaweed burger.

I think the company overreacted to a small segment of self-appointed food cops who probably never ate at its restaurants. (And if they did, they wouldn't admit it.)

I'm not saying that the fast-food industry shouldn't develop healthier hamburgers. I'm saying that people won't buy low-fat alternatives unless they are a reasonable facsimile of the real thing. If all I could eat was a McLean Deluxe, I'd give up hamburgers altogether.

At the same time that McDonald's killed McLean Deluxe, it was testing the Arch Deluxe, a huge burger with bacon. Meanwhile, other chains were offering new calorie-laden treats. Taco Bell's Double-Decker taco and Pizza Hut's Triple-Decker pizza were selling like gangbusters. Fast-food consumers wanted these products. McLean Deluxe—and similar "healthy" foods at other chains—were products that only critics who don't buy fast-food meals could love.

People can talk all they want about eating healthier. And they will. Develop products for them. But don't bet against fast-food restaurants until you see them being boarded up as quickly as they're now being constructed.

A whole generation of fast-food addicts has come of age. For better or worse, fatty burgers, fries, and tacos are the standards against which future culinary efforts will be tested. You can lead consumers to a healthy meal. But unless it tastes as good as the fatty fast food they're used to, they won't eat it.

As for me, I'll have a salad for lunch. But what I

really crave—are you listening, Dave?—is a Quadruple-Decker Wendy's Burger.

GULP!

That's often the last sound that's heard when a big conglomerate swallows up an innovative entrepreneur. Either that, or the ghastly rumbles of indigestion, as happened following Quaker Oats Company's $1.7 billion purchase of Snapple, the line of New Age beverages. It wound up selling Snapple for $300 million just three years later.

Some small brands are lucky enough to get all the distribution clout and marketing muscle they were promised by their suitors, of course, and they thrive as a result. But it's very difficult for a large company to maintain the culture that made many small companies successful.

Celestial Seasonings comes immediately to mind. Mo Siegel, a carefree hippie, started the herbal tea company in 1972 with his wife and two friends by borrowing $10,000. Everything about Celestial Seasonings was idiosyncratic: the product itself, the psychedelic packaging with corny aphorisms, the nontraditional way the company was run. Then, in 1984, Kraft Foods bought Celestial Seasonings for $36 million. It imposed a dress code, insisted on rigorous market testing before it launched new flavors, and thought about ways to extend the brand name into salad dressings and the like. In other words, it tried to make Celestial Seasonings a Kraft division. Mercifully, a venture capital firm bought Celestial Seasonings back from Kraft before it was totally consumed by soulless MBAs.

That's not really fair, of course. Big companies work on economies of scale that make it impossible for them to nurture small businesses the way that their founders did. And often there's just not enough potential for profit for top management to devote enough time or energy to running the acquisition properly. I learned this firsthand in 1967 when I took over a small importing company in the United States that was selling the Goddard line of polishes and cleaning aids. Goddard was a British company that held the Royal Warrant, which means, among other things, that its products were used to polish the Queen's silver.

I knew the specialty marketing approach from observing the work my father did as I grew up. Dad had developed Halo Shampoo and sold it to Colgate. He also marketed Angel Skin, a skin cream that he sold to Ponds. I felt that there were ways of romancing American consumers into a relationship with an aristocratic-sounding English company.

Initially, there were four polishes. Over time, I helped to develop thirty-two additional products. Most of what we marketed in the United States was different from what Goddard marketed in the United Kingdom. I developed the business from less than $1,000 a month in sales to more than $150,000.

Because Goddard was a family company, with all the airs of English gentlemen who play by the rules of fairness, I thought I was secure for the rest of my career. But I ran afoul of an old problem: The son of the company's chairman didn't want to take over what his great-grandfather had started and his dad had been running. The Goddard family decided to cash out. I hadn't the slightest inkling of what its plans were until

I was abruptly asked to resign from the board of directors.

"I am selling the company the first of next month," Herald Goddard simply told me.

Goddard sold the operation to an American company, S.C. Johnson & Son, Inc., which itself has been a paternalistic family business since it was founded in 1886. Samuel C. Johnson, a carpenter in Racine, Wisconsin, developed his company after inventing a wax for parquet. S.C. Johnson & Son had never laid off an employee or had a strike. It donated 5 percent of its pretax profits to charity. And over the years, it had been a new-product innovator. In the mid-fifties, it introduced Raid bug spray. Later, it developed Off! insecticide. Both are leaders in their categories. The Johnson R&D lab has also given us Pledge furniture polish, Edge shaving cream, and Agree shampoo, among other products.

Johnson was attracted to Goddard, its executives later told me, because of what I had done with the line in the United States. If I had single-handedly goosed sales to $150,000 a month, they could take it into the "millions," they felt. Johnson kept me on board after it took over.

One of the first things Johnson did was move its new subsidiary from Goddard's very modern factory in Leicester to its own very modern factory in Frimly Green. The only difference was that the new plant was designed for quantity, not quality. Forget about new products. The highly mechanized and bureaucratic Johnson system could not keep up with my orders for existing business. At one point, for instance, I needed silver brushes. Unfortunately, "the computer" forgot to order the handles for the brushes. It placed the orders for the bristles, the labels, and the boxes, but when the time came to put it all together, the handles were missing. Sometimes the plant in England had to resort to air-shipping my products to make deadlines. I had to pay the extra shipping costs, of course. Ever try to airfreight cases of 15-ounce silver polish and still make enough profit to feed a growing family? I learned that it can't be done. And Johnson eventually learned, long after I left to seek my fortune elsewhere, that some of the techniques that work in introducing new products to the mass market can't be successfully transferred to premium markets where customers are cultivated by delivering quality and reliability.

Several years after I'd left, a Johnson vice president contacted me to see if I wanted to take over the business again. I politely declined. Goddard's sales had plummeted to around $200,000 annually.

What's the moral? It depends on your perspective. If you're an executive with a large company, beware of acquiring small brands that have been successful precisely because they are small enough to be quirky (and quirky enough to be small). If you're an entrepreneur with a quirky brand, by all means take the money and run. And if you're an employee or independent contractor intent on staying on, as I was, forget about it. Get those résumés in the mail.

H

HONEST FAILURE

It's a shame that we have no system for rewarding honest failure in America. And that we have such a hard time being honest with ourselves. We squander a lot of money pretending that we're winners. We build houses of cards, movie-set facades, empty shells. I can't tell you how many times I've heard about a family that mortgages itself to the hilt for a home in a prestigious area. The inside of their house is empty, though, because there's no money left for furnishings.

We've created a management environment that rewards people for constructing facades and ignoring reality. You have to pretend, even if it's not true, that you are better, bigger, stronger, faster-acting, newer, and more improved than everybody else. Second place doesn't suffice in our culture. There's a do-or-die passion to be Number One.

Most of the time, though, we're not Number One. We just fudge the facts and pretend to be.

Baseball manager Leo Durocher once said that "nice guys finish last." In most bureaucracies, honest people finish last—unless what's honest happens to coincide with what the boss wants to hear.

As a result, mid-level managers who are responsible for conducting market tests are reluctant to relay bad news to upper management. Once a company has invested tens of thousands, even millions, of dollars developing a product, it's difficult to tell bosses that the product is a bomb. So employees hem and haw. They hatch excuses for the performance of the product in test. They make unrealistic projections for it in the real world. As a result, the product is brought to the full market, where it proceeds to lose millions of dollars more.

Let your people know that bad news is just as welcome as good news, as long as it's based on solid facts. And don't be afraid to reward honest failure. Give a whopping bonus to the person who tells you something you really don't want to hear. It may be the most prudent investment you'll ever make.

HOT BUTTONS FOR SUCCESS IN THE MILLENNIUM

Innovative products that meet consumers' needs in one or more of the following areas have a better than average chance of success, and I expect these areas to remain hot right into the third millennium. There are chapters on each of these areas (some you've already read and the others follow), but I'm compiling them here for your convenience.

- Convenience
- Environment
- Ethnicity
- Fun
- Nutrition
- Packaging

- Size
- Youth

One word of caution: All the marketing fundamentals still apply. A vitamin-fortified granola bar simply packed in recycled paper that kids like to eat because it makes a cool crunching sound when they bite it may be loaded with positive attributes. When you get down to it, though, the make-or-break attribute for food is taste. If that bar doesn't pass kids' no-nonsense taste test, it will flop.

I

ICE CUBES TO COCKER SPANIELS

Selling ice cubes to Eskimos is an overrated marketing feat. It's done all the time. When someone asks a waiter for an Evian instead of a perfectly fine glass of tap water, he's an Eskimo buying ice cubes.

Selling ice cubes to cocker spaniels is a whole different story. Let's get over the first hump. Cocker spaniels do have a sizable amount of income at their disposal. It goes for food, shots, rubber balls, bones, flea collars, teeth cleanings, and silly reindeer antlers at Christmastime. But cocker spaniels will not spend their masters' hard-earned money on store-bought ice cubes. They have absolutely no use for them. I don't need a marketing study to back me up on that.

It's amazing to me how many marketers try to sell ice cubes to cocker spaniels. Take R.J. Reynolds, for instance. It has spent a fortune trying to develop a smokeless cigarette. Smokeless cigarettes appeal to nonsmokers. Nonsmokers don't buy cigarettes.

The tobacco companies are in a peculiar situation. Not since patent medicines were effectively banned at the turn of the twentieth century has such a popular, profitable product faced such an uncertain future. Competitive products are not the main barrier to tobacco products' continued success. Their nemesis is people who do not smoke and who vehemently express their distaste for those who do.

The tobacco industry has tried to mute its critics in many ways, ranging from public-relations campaigns that support the "rights" of smokers to averring there is no scientific proof that secondhand smoke is damaging to nonsmokers. They also have spent an awful lot of money developing and trying to market cigarettes that would be less offensive to nonsmokers. This has never made sense to me. Why create a product for a consumer who wants absolutely nothing to do with you?

I've never heard a nonsmoker say to a cigarette smoker, "If you *must* smoke in my presence, please use Brand X, which is more pleasing to smell." Some people do profess that they like the scent of a good cigar or pipe tobacco. I suspect, however, that it has something to do with a subconscious association with memories of a loved one—a father or favorite uncle—relaxing and enjoying what is, no doubt, a gratifying experience to many people.

Reynolds flopped big time—it reportedly lost $325 million—with its introduction of Premier cigarettes in the late 1980s. Reynolds's own president felt that Premier cigarettes "tasted like crap." While no amount of marketing can overcome a handicap like that, taste wasn't the only thing wrong with Premier. In fact, it was a cigarette that only someone who hated cigarettes could love, as I told David Letterman during an appearance on his TV show.

First, it was difficult to light. So difficult, in fact, that when Letterman held a flame to one, he was moved to ask, "What's the deal with the lighter? That's not working either."

Second, it did not generate any ash. Reynolds's researchers reportedly had "discovered" that smokers like to have something to do with their hands. I suppose that's why they tried to make Premier as close to a cigarette as possible instead of, for example, injecting a dollop of nicotine into a sweet gumball. But watch a smoker sometime. You'll discover that each smoker has a ritual way of dealing with the ash on the tip of a cigarette, whether it's gently rubbing it off on the side of the ashtray, repeatedly pounding the cigarette with the index finger, or letting it accumulate until it dribbles off onto the clothing (the absentminded-professor routine). Whatever the technique, the smoker is doing something with his or her hand. Disposing of the ash is an integral part of the smoking experience.

Third, smokers like to be wreathed in smoke. I don't know why, but they do. Maybe it's comforting—perhaps smoke is a vapory security blanket that evokes the warmth of the hearth. Smoke also can be mysterious, even sexy. Think of Marlene Dietrich or Humphrey Bogart enveloped in a hazy cloud.

Finally, social pressures aside, you can't expect

someone to shell out money for a product that does not satisfy the urge to buy it. The smell of Premier was not gratifying to anybody.

"It's like standing near a smoldering trash fire," Letterman said.

It amazes me that even after the Premier debacle, Reynolds has continued to develop a product that in my opinion smokers will not want. According to published reports, Reynolds has spent many millions developing a brand called Eclipse that heats charcoal to extract the flavor from the tobacco. Again, the cigarette generates little ash. Nicotine levels are about the same as with conventional cigarettes, making it just as addictive, but the tar level is greatly reduced.

Spokespeople for Reynolds, while emphasizing that the cigarette might never be rolled out nationally, claimed that it is very popular in tests with both smokers and nonsmoking spouses and family members. That may be. But even if it doesn't "taste like crap," as Premier did, I doubt that the smokeless cigarette will do any better than beers containing less than 0.5 percent alcohol have done. Although nonalcohol beers, as the industry calls them, have developed a niche, most beer drinkers scorn the very idea of a beer without a kick.

One thing that nonalcohol beer has going for it that a smokeless cigarette doesn't is that it's truly a healthy alternative to imbibing too much alcohol. Critics of Eclipse, on the other hand, charge that the product is nothing more than a nicotine-delivery system and want it regulated by the Food and Drug Administration.

As I write, Eclipse has been pulled from test. If it should be revived, I think we'll see another pile of Reynolds's greenbacks go up in smokeless.

IMAGE, EVEN IF IT'S ANTI-IMAGE, IS EVERYTHING

Each man, woman, and child in the United States drinks about 122 gallons of nonalcoholic beverages other than tap water and vegetable juice each year. Adults guzzle an additional 37 gallons of beer, wine, and hard liquor. We cannot survive without frequently replenishing the combination of hydrogen and oxygen that fills two-thirds of our bodies. But no physician has ever suggested that we must drink Gatorade, Bartles & Jaymes coolers, Snapple iced tea, Diet Coke, Juicy Juice, Barq's root beer, Tropicana orange juice, Kool Aid, Miller Lite, Absolut, Fruitopia, Perrier, Nestlé's chocolate milk, or Sanka brand decaffeinated coffee.

The marketing of beverages offers as clear an insight into good and bad marketing as any one category can. Everybody drinks liquids. Nobody *has to* drink branded liquids. In reality, people drink the marketing.

Maxwell House is "Good to the Last Drop." "Coke Is It" (except when New Coke was introduced in 1986, a momentary gaffe that suggested that Coke as we'd come to love it was "Not It" after all). Perrier is "Earth's First Soft Drink." Sometimes the tag line is visual, such as the sketch of a smiling face on a bulging Kool Aid pitcher or the bosomy babes in most beer commercials.

People drink the image and positioning of a beverage product. Even when it is an anti-image.

Billboards for Sprite in the mid-1990s told the young adults it was targeting that "Image is nothing, thirst is everything, obey your thirst." A Sprite television commercial proclaimed, "Drink what tastes good because television can make anything taste good." Then it showed a glass of cola that was actually cod liver oil.

This cynical "anti-advertising" was executed with humor to soften the edge. It was a total reversal of Sprite's prior positioning. Before the irreverent "obey your thirst" campaign began, Sprite's advertising was as upbeat as most soft-drink ads. It included words like "clear," "sparkling," and "unique." It had the requisite sappy slogan: "I like the Sprite in you." It even had an animated "lymon" at one point. But Sprite's cheery image wasn't appealing to young soda drinkers in the nineties.

The new image of Sprite really has nothing to do with the drink itself and everything to do with the current attitude of the group it is trying to seduce.

"We're saying you, the consumer, know what's cool," said an executive at the ad agency that created the Sprite ads. "You can't define cool in the ads because if you do, it's no longer cool."*

That's a very nineties concept.

Beverage advertising has very little to do with the product. It has everything to do with its drinkers, or

*Lee Garfinkel, co-chairman and chief creative officer of Lowe & Partners/SMS, as quoted in *The New York Times*, "Nice-Guy Sprite Gets an Attitude as Coca-Cola Pursues Irreverent, Playful Young Consumers," July 25, 1995.

the people it covets as drinkers. Image is, in fact, everything—even if the image is "image is nothing."

It has always been that way.

If you don't believe me, pick up a package of Postum at your local supermarket. Brew some. Sip it. Then explain to me how something that tastes so dreadful could have been so popular in my grandparents' day.

The reason is simple. Postum was positioned as a healthy alternative to coffee in advertising so scary that it would make Juan Valdez swear off caffeine. But the scary images in Postum ads grew tamer and lamer over the years, before disappearing altogether. (There's no mystery why such a strong image was left out to dry. Its parent company, which is now Kraft Foods, became the world's biggest coffee marketer.)

Define your image. Obey your image. Image is everything.

IF ONLY YOU COULD BOTTLE ...

Some products I see remind me of the phrase "If only you could bottle little Billy's energy and sell it, you'd make a fortune." They are basically good products, but they will never make a fortune because they haven't been packaged properly.

BBQ Buddies is such a product. I was immediately attracted to the idea of pulling a trigger and spraying barbecue sauce on McMath's Famous Barbecued Spareribs (just ask my neighbors about them). Spraying is much easier than slathering on sauce with a brush or spoon. BBQ Buddies is also fun to use, and prevents the short hairs on the back of your hand from being singed by flaring coals. Unfortunately, the BBQ Buddies container is so tall that retailers must store it way up on the top shelf, out of sight of people who are shorter than my six feet five inches. The plastic bottle only fits in my refrigerator if I lay it on its side, and it's equally difficult to store in a cabinet. Even worse, perhaps, is that the bottle looks like it was made to hold window cleanser rather than a tasty condiment. Yuck. A distinctive, more compact container would help this product catch fire.

Speaking about cleaning products, Colgate-Palmolive created a two-headed monster with its Short Cut Double Duty Cleanser. It was sold in a blue plastic bottle that looked like a liquid laundry detergent container. On the top was a push-down sprayer; on the side was a screw-top opening. The idea was that consumers could spray Short Cut for light cleaning jobs such as wiping a counter, or they could pour it out and mix it with water for heavier tasks such as mopping the floor. Unfortunately, the Short Cut container tended to leak. The wadding that sealed the opening of the screw-top part of the container was the same kind of material used in normal bottles, but the liquid in a normal bottle only hits the seal occasionally—when someone tips it to read the label, for instance. But because the spout of Short Cut's bottle was on the side, the liquid was in constant contact with the wadding material, and eventually ate through it. Sometimes the bottle leaked on the store shelves, sometimes in transit (you can imagine shoppers' reactions when they found a bagful of groceries soaked with Short Cut), and sometimes in homes.

Short Cut's novel design was supposed to make consumers' lives easier. In practice, however, it often created a mess.

On the other side of the coin, some products are winners primarily because they are packaged so perfectly. So much so that I simply need to tell you the names and you'll know exactly what I'm talking about. L'Eggs. Tic-Tacs. Popsicle. Slim Jim. Hostess Cup Cake. Reach toothbrush. Mentadent. And let's not forget that all-time classic, the fluted Coca-Cola bottle.

Your package must be attractive, eye-catching, and appropriate to the product. But don't forget the basics. It must be functional, too.

IS THERE A MARKET FOR YOUR PRODUCT?

I can't tell you how many times I've seen people at trade shows who are filled with excitement about a product they're introducing that's made from a recipe that has been in their family for generations. They feel their product can't miss because every Tom, Deb, and Harry who has ever come into their home has raved about it. What else would they say? Even if their friends and relatives sincerely adored their Six-Alarm Chili, it doesn't mean that they—or anyone else—would buy it at the Shop Rite.

Some markets never seem to materialize no matter how good the product or technology appears on the surface:

• Food packaged in tubes, which is a convenience that's popular in many countries including Canada, has failed to catch on in the United States.

- The telephone companies have envisioned a video phone in every household for more than a half-century, but consumers just don't see the need for it.

- Sony's Betacam technology was superior to the VCR technology now standard in American households, but it was outproduced and outmarketed.

- And, inexplicably as far as I'm concerned, English crumpets have never caught on in this country. If properly toasted and served with butter and a touch of strawberry jam, they are more scrumptious than English muffins and nowhere near as dry as scones. (Scone mixes, by the way, are the rage at trade shows, even though most Americans have no idea what they are and have little incentive to find out since there is a tastier alternative—I'm thinking here of a nice, fat jelly doughnut—sold at every mall and Main Street.)

Almost every week I receive a call from someone who wants advice about how to sell a secret recipe to a large company. I recall one woman in particular who insisted that General Foods (now subsumed by Kraft Foods) could make a fortune off her grandmother's bread-pudding recipe. She would divulge the ingredients to General Foods, she said, for a mere $100,000. And 25 percent of the profit. She thought I was nuts for telling her that her financial demands were unreasonable, and I had a terrible time explaining that no matter how tasty her bread pudding was, most people would have no interest in eating it and General Foods would have no interest in buying it. No matter how you slice it, Bread Pudding-O just isn't Jell-O.

Without a market, you don't have a product.

I'M THE BOSS, THAT'S WHY

After I graduated from Johns Hopkins University, I accepted a position in the toiletries division of the Colgate-Palmolive Company. The company, which was founded in 1806, was already a global marketing power-house in the 1950s. Some of its leading brands were quite different from today's, however. The toiletries division was responsible for everything from Colgate Dental Cream (with Gardol!) to Veto Deodorant. Veto, with a cute bulbous spray bottle that people just "loved to squeeze," was one of the leading deodorant/anti-perspirants at the time. Now it doesn't exist, but that's another story.

As a sharp, eager young marketer, I was assigned the task of developing a new package and image for Palmolive After Shave Lotion, which had a beautiful dark-green color and sold for a buck. It came in a molded, hand-size bottle. This was back in the days when drugstores were the biggest purveyors of men's toiletries. They put out large displays of aftershave lotions on their counters and often featured the lotions in their windows. For a price, of course. Manufacturers "purchased" the display window, or part of it, each merchandise period. Sometimes we paid cash; some-times we threw in extra merchandise.

Standing alone, Palmolive After Shave's deep green color looked rich and classy. But when it was displayed next to its chief competitor, Mennen Skin Bracer, it looked as if someone had used the bottle for a urinal. Against the crisp, clean-looking blue of Mennen, the green took on a sickly yellowish hue. Needless to say, it lost its appeal to the impulse buyer.

Annual sales for the line amounted to only about $1 million—enough for you or me, thank you, but not enough for Colgate. Management wanted it fixed or killed.

I plunged right into the assignment. I went to the Colgate laboratories and, with all the resolve of a young hotshot, told them I wanted a nonfugitive blue color for the lotion. That means that I wanted a blue that wouldn't fade even if it were exposed to the intense sunlight of a window display. Then I went to the packaging department. Together we developed a beautiful shadow box with a gold edge on the open front that highlighted the rectangular bottle, which you could see through the opening. The bottle had gold graphics and a gold cap. It was beautiful.

Then I took the finished prototype to my boss, the merchandise manager for the toiletries division, with high hopes and in high spirits. He liked what he saw. He, in turn, took it to the vice president in charge of the toiletries division. This was my introduction to the vagaries of success and failure in the corporate world.

It turned out that the man who held the life-or-death decision over my work didn't like the color blue. Not just "my" color blue. *Any* color blue. Azure. Sky. Royal. Turquoise. Navy. He didn't wear blue suits. He didn't wear blue ties, or blue coats, or drive a blue car. There was nothing blue in his office. The word that came back to me was, simply, "He *hates* the color blue." End of project. End of product.

We'll never know if a repackaged Palmolive After Shave lotion would have succeeded or not, but Mennen's aftershave is still doing very well. Then again,

Colgate now owns the Mennen company, which is itself a general lesson in corporate behavior. I, however, chose to take a particular lesson out of the experience, one that perhaps launched me on the road to learning from my defeats. Right then and there I vowed that if ever I got into a position of responsibility, I would not pigheadedly insist that my personal tastes prevail over well-reasoned strategies.

J

JUMPING ON THE TREND WAGON

When sales for a hot new product surge, it's natural to think that a long-term trend is underway. More often than not, though, it's a short-lived fad.

The wine-cooler explosion of the 1980s is a perfect example. Dozens of companies lost money by jumping on the trend wagon after two college buddies introduced a mixture of white wine, citrus juice, carbonated water, and fructose called California Cooler. The sweet concoction tapped into a demographic gold mine. The generation that had grown up drinking soda pop and Kool Aid had reached the prime age for alcohol consumption. Sweet California Cooler was a quick hit with young people, particularly women, who didn't like the taste of beer but who wanted an alcoholic drink that was refreshing and could be guzzled.

Dozens of companies, from backyard entrepreneurs to Anheuser-Busch, rushed into the market with me-too products. I counted more than 150 wine-cooler brands by 1985. There were many varieties—exotic fruit flavors, different percentages of alcohol content—but to consumers it looked like an endless stream of Tweedle-Dum and Tweedle-Dumber.

The California Cooler entrepreneurs wisely sold their company to Brown-Forman Corporation, the makers of Jack Daniel's whiskey and other brands, at the height of the wine-cooler frenzy. They became instant millionaires. Their brand fared less well. California Cooler was eventually obliterated by two experienced alcohol marketers, Gallo and Seagram, who blitzed the airwaves with high-impact commercials. They left few surviving wine-cooler brands in their wake.

The quick success of wine coolers was clearly a case of young people imbibing the hype. Once they sampled the beverage, in all its varieties, most decided that wine coolers were just too sweet for frequent consumption. The market today is a sliver of what dozens of marketers, from beverage behemoths to backyard entrepreneurs, hoped it would become.

Look hard before you jump onto the trend wagon. Inevitably, as more players get into the market, a competitive battle ensues. Stores charge higher slotting fees. Advertising and promotion spending gets heavier. Margins disappear as prices drop. Undercapitalized brands wither and die. Almost everybody loses money. And nine times out of ten, the trend turns out to have been a fad.

KID STUFF

One quick way to a kid's stomach is to license the rights to the latest, greatest Disney character or ride the coattails of the season's hot PG movie. But the best kind of marketing to kids transcends short-term licensing deals. Indeed, it transcends generations.

A forty-something friend of mine who swears by his grandmother's recipe for homemade macaroni and cheese discovered Kraft's famous blue box version of the meal only recently. The introduction was made by his eight-year-old daughter's classmate, who was sleeping over at their home. The girl's mother, sagely planning ahead for the inevitable complaint that "[fill-in-the-blank] taste yucky and I won't eat 'em," packed a box of the Bugs Bunny and Friends version of the pasta in her duffel bag. Not only did the little girl prepare her Kraft Macaroni & Cheese Dinner by herself, she also regaled the family with a commentary on its yumminess. Although my friend still prefers his grandma's home-cooked recipe, his daughter is a convert to Kraft. And his wife is, too. Grandma's recipe is a lot more work to prepare.

Back in the late 1930s, Kraft advertised Macaroni & Cheese Dinner as "a meal for four in nine minutes for an everyday price of nineteen cents." This straight-forward appeal to Depression-era housewives trying to stretch their food dollars has been superseded by some of the most clever marketing to children I've ever seen. The pasta is molded into other figures popular with kids, such as dinosaurs (Cheesasaurus Rex), the Flintstones, and teddy bears. The colorful packaging, always with a blue backdrop, possesses cereal-box pizzazz. Kids are invited to join a Kraft Cheese & Macaroni Club—a reversal of the two words in the brand name to emphasize that it's the "cheesiest" choice possible. Other promotions include a custom-made comic book, "Cheesasaurus Rex and the Kraft Cheese & Macaroni Friends," and a TV sweepstakes in which kids were asked to write a "happenin'" rap song about their favorite Kraft Macaroni & Cheese version.

Sure, Kraft spends big bucks in licensing fees. But Macaroni & Cheese Dinner has been successful for more than sixty years primarily because Kraft understands both of its constituencies—parents looking for an economical, easy-to-prepare meal, and kids who aren't bashful about begging, wheedling, or cajoling their parents for brands that they find tasty. For all the marketing excitement that Kraft creates around the brand, it relies on the most evangelical of salespeople—kids themselves—to close the sale.

KILLER CLERKS

Watch out for killer clerks. They can fritter away all the goodwill you invest in your product. A few clerks are naturally malicious. Some—consumer electronics is notorious for this—are paid "spiffs" to push a brand. Others are poorly supervised. Most are poorly trained.

Killer clerks are everywhere, particularly the supermarket, where stocking shelves is not much different than it was in Mr. Whipple's heyday. Don't get too fancy with supermarket clerks.

Campbell's Fresh Chef was a fresh, prepared pasta and vegetable salad and soup line that was sold in the dairy case. It was packaged in a jar. When clerks restocked the shelves, they did not treat it like other dairy items such as milk. Instead, they often pushed the older stock to the back, as they do with shelf-stable canned and jarred goods. It didn't help that the pull date was hard to find on the label. Try as it might, Campbell could not get the clerks to properly rotate the perishable stock.

The Chillery salad line from Kraft suffered a similar fate. Chillery salads (pastas, shrimp, and the like) were packaged in plastic containers. They came with a stand-alone, chilled display case. If a clerk saw empty space in the case, he filled it with something. Anything, in fact. Marie's Salad Dressing. Claussen's Pickles. Display cases were often more than half-filled with products other than Chillery.

Campbell and Kraft were not experienced in the fresh-produce business. They tried to introduce a new way of doing things to clerks who were set in their ways. The fresh-salad brands that have been successful since then—Dole, Salad Time, and Fresh Express to name three—come from companies that have been longtime players in the produce business. They made sure that their channel of distribution, from the packers to the clerks, knew how to handle their products.

Killer clerks don't lurk only beside the okra and kale, of course. They leer behind the cash register. They linger behind the counter. You may not get clerks working with you. But be damn sure that they're not working against you. When you introduce something new, keep it simple and easy for them to understand.

L

LOYALTY: YOUR ONLY EQUITY

Some consultants have taken to rating the value of brand names as if they were absolute statistics, like a pitcher's earned run average. They call this Brand Equity. These ratings make for nice magazine cover stories. Brand names such as Disney, Coke, and Kodak are always near the top. So is Marlboro.

But brands' overall worth can't be measured precisely in dollars and cents. They are much richer (or poorer) than their stats. Forget sales volume (or share of market), too. The true worth of each brand is the sum of the loyalty of its consumers.

If someone offered you the choice of a Meiji, a leading Japanese chocolate bar, and a Hershey bar, you'd pick Hershey (unless you're Japanese or in a mood to try something different). Both Hershey and Meiji are worth millions of dollars independent of the value of the machines that make them and the real estate their factories occupy.

But both Hershey and Meiji are, in and of themselves, worthless.

What's valuable is the loyalty of their customers. Hershey is valuable as long as its customers believe it's valuable.

There are few relationships in life that are as fragile as loyalty, whether it's between nations, friends, or family. As long as a relationship continues the way it always has, loyalty remains steadfast. But when new elements are introduced—a government changes; a good friend gets married—relationships are apt to change.

If you change your brand in some way, you run the risk of undermining all the trust you've built up over the years.

I'm not advocating that you sit on your success. "New" and "improved" are probably the most overworked words in the annals of copywriting, and deservedly so. Nothing's perfect. We all accept that there's always room for improvement. Technology advances. Formulas improve. Marketing must keep pace with the times.

But be very careful about how you do it.

Coca-Cola committed the biggest formulation fiasco in marketing history when it changed the taste of its flagship brand in 1986. When a national brouhaha erupted, Coke executives claimed that consumers preferred the new formula in blind taste tests. True. But the taste-testers were not told that the Coke they'd known and loved all their lives would be dumped in favor of the new formula. Coke brought back its "Classic" formula fast enough to avoid a total rebellion of its loyalists.

Schlitz was not as adept. Schlitz made the best-selling beer in the United States as recently as the 1970s. Then it changed its formula so that the beer would brew faster. Beer drinkers hated the new taste. By the time the reformulation was reformulated, the brand was in a tailspin from which it could not recover.

One study estimates that it costs four to six times more to convert a customer than it does to retain one. Another concluded that companies can almost double their profits by retaining just 5 percent more of their customers.*

In your rush to improve or innovate, never forget that your most valuable asset is the loyalty of your existing customers.

LOW EXPECTATIONS

What if the Big Mac had been named the Little Mac? The Eveready battery was the Oftenready? Charmin Tissues were "reasonably" soft?

People would not expect much from these products. They wouldn't buy them either. Consumers want you to make big, bold promises. If you include a benefit in a product name or tag line, never waffle or waver.

A generation ago, bad-hair days seemed epidemic. Women frequently complained, "I just shampooed my hair, and I can't do a thing with it." They moved from brand to brand looking for a miracle. A *big* miracle. That was the problem with Clairol's Small Miracle. Women had gigantic expectations. Clairol made a small promise.

If you're going to promise a miracle, you may as well go all the way.

---

*The points are made in *The Fourth Wave: Brand Loyalty Marketing* (New York: Coalition for Brand Equity, 1994). Authors Larry Light and Richard Morgan claim that "brand loyalty marketing" is the natural successor to the outdated concepts of mass marketing, target marketing, and global marketing.

LET SLEEPING DOGS DIE

"I'll take a Sanka."

Not too many years ago, that's what you'd tell your waiter if you wanted a decaffeinated coffee. There was little else available. And even if you didn't want it, Sanka was what you'd get. It often was served unmixed, the orange-and-brown packet sitting on a saucer with a cup of hot water. In finer restaurants, they'd mix it for you in the kitchen. Because of its distinctive medicinal flavor, however, after a single sip you'd know you were drinking Sanka instant. Restaurants hardly ever brewed decaf by the pot because there was not enough demand. And there were not too many brands.

Sanka was once so dominant in its category, in fact, that it came perilously close to becoming a generic term. Advertisements referred to it as "Sanka Brand Decaffeinated Coffee" to protect it from becoming a thermos or band-aid or kleenex. (Attention corporate lawyers: for the record, that's "Thermos®," "Band-Aid®," and "Kleenex®.")

That was then. Today people simply say, "I'll have a decaf." Often they're served a freshly brewed cup of a specialty coffee that's decaffeinated but tastes just as good as regular java. When they're not, they're more often served a different brand than Sanka unless they ask for it. Excuse me. It's now known as Maxwell House® Sanka®.

Sanka has been around as a ground coffee since 1903, and as an instant since just after World War II. It pretty much had the category to itself until consumers became health conscious in the late 1960s. As drinking decaffeinated coffee became more popular, competition came not only from instant varieties but also from fresh-brewed brands and specialty blends. Every restaurant today, even a greasy spoon, has a pot of decaf on the burner.

On the one hand, Sanka is testimony to how far the mighty can fall, proof that no product is invincible to trends and improved products. In truth, however, there was very little that Sanka's marketers could do about it. And probably little that they should.

Sanka is still a very profitable franchise, particularly with older coffee drinkers who acquired a taste for it (and still have fond memories of the commercials starring Robert Young, everybody's favorite TV father and medical doctor). In fact, as recently as 1994, Sanka was the leading instant decaf brand in supermarkets measured by dollar sales, according to Information Resources, Inc., although Nestlé's Taster's Choice and Procter & Gamble's Folgers decaffeinated blends were right behind it and moving up fast.

Clearly Sanka does not have a perky future. In Total Research Corporation's annual EquiTrend survey of brand quality from 1990 to 1994, Americans consistently placed Sanka near the bottom of a list of 200 popular products as diverse as Disney World (#1 in 1994) and Advil (#49). Sanka was #196 in 1994, finishing just above store-brand photographic film and store-brand cola. When a once-sizzling brand name is ranked that close to generic products that are primarily bought because of their lower prices, its future is behind it.

I certainly think that some venerable brands can

and should be rejuvenated (see *Some Things Old Can Be New Again*). But you've got to carefully assess your strengths in deciding whether it's worth the effort. Sanka has only one real benefit. It is without caffeine, as its name—a contraction of the French phrase *sans caffeine*—proclaims. The only reason to drink it is because it's missing something. To most palates, however, it's missing two things: caffeine and real-coffee flavor. Nowadays, most decaf coffees are indistinguishable in taste from regular java.

It's beyond me why Kraft Foods folded Sanka into its Maxwell House line. Maxwell House is, of course, locked in a perennial battle with Folgers for the title of King of the Coffees. Was it to add a few market-share points? If so, that's a bad reason. Maxwell House is a strong brand with a reputation of "Good to the Last Drop" to maintain. Sanka's taste—particularly the instant variety that most people think about when they hear the name—does not support that tag line.

If you've got a sleeping dog like Sanka, let it die a natural death. Treat it, and its loyal customers, with the dignity and respect they deserve. Distribute it widely. Support it minimally. Milk it for all the profit you can. Meanwhile, create new products that address its shortcomings, and build new brands for the future.

ME-TOO MADNESS

Me-too me-too me-too me-too me-too me-too me-too marketing is the number one killer of new products.

The second me-too in that sentence is superfluous. The third, fourth, fifth, and all the rest are downright foolish. So are most "new" products because they are nothing more than blatant knockoffs of existing brands.

Most attempts at me-too marketing fail. The ones that succeed usually require resources and persistence that are beyond the capabilities of most marketers. Pepsi-Cola led a very precarious existence for decades before establishing itself as the major competitor to Coca-Cola. More to the point, though, is that Pepsi is one of the few survivors among dozens of other brands that have challenged Coke for more than a century. Ever hear of Toca-Cola? Coco-Cola? Yum-Yum cola? French Wine of Cola? How about King-Cola, "the royal drink"? Or Coca Ree, "the ideal brain food"? Those were early casualties. More recently, Afri Cola failed to attract African-American soda drinkers, and Cajun Cola pretty well flopped in the land of gumbo. I could go on and on, but you get the point.

All things being equal, an established product has a

distinct advantage over any new product that is not radically different from it. There are several ways to level the playing field, but all of them involve having very deep pockets (see *McMath's Five Rules of Me-Too Marketing Success* below).

The most obvious is to spend a lot of money on advertising or promotion. That's how Crest toothpaste got started in 1955 and eventually toppled Colgate for the market lead. The American Dental Association endorsed the effectiveness of Crest's fluoride formula, but what really sold consumers were ubiquitous commercials with the tag line "Look mom, no cavities!" Crest continues to dominate the category in the 1990s thanks to $60 to $75 million worth of annual advertising.

Marketers also can leverage an existing brand name to give a product instant credibility in the minds of consumers. That's why there are so many varieties of Crest today, from Crest with mint flavor to Crest for sensitive teeth. I'm not advocating me-too brand extensions for reasons I've already made clear (see *Extensions: Why They're Bad*), but they can be a daunting and formidable force in the marketplace. The retail price of Sensodyne, the innovator of toothpaste for people with sensitive teeth, is much higher than that of Crest's me-too extension. Sensodyne will either have to cut its price or lose substantial market share.

Finally, marketers can do things the old-fashioned way by creating an innovative product that actually fills a need. In the early 1980s, for example, periodontists began to tell patients with gum disease to brush with a mixture of baking soda and hydrogen peroxide.

Hand-mixing the ingredients was a long, messy process that many consumers avoided. Then Arm & Hammer created a toothpaste that contained its market-leading baking soda. Other manufacturers followed with their me-too versions. These products did not contain hydrogen peroxide, however. Finally, Chesebrough-Pond's introduced Mentadent Toothpaste. Mentadent is contained in an unusual double container. When the consumer pushes on the plunger, baking soda and peroxide are mixed. This innovative product quickly became one of the top-selling toothpastes, and continues to be very successful. It commands a premium price because it fills a need and is a demonstrably better product.

McMath's Five Rules of Me-Too Marketing Success

1. You must have a demonstrably better product—or you must be able to make consumers believe that you have a demonstrably better product—than the market leader.

2. You must spend enough money in advertising and promotion to make consumers aware of your demonstrably better product.

3. You must convince retailers that you will spend enough money in advertising and promotion to keep consumers aware of your product.

4. You must be prepared to spend more money than the competition to assure sufficient shelf space for your product.

5. You must be able to withstand a price war, which may continue for years, during which your profits will be negligible.

Remember, me-too marketing is the number one killer of products because most me-too products deserve to die. Unfortunately, the innovator in a category is often the victim if the knockoff product has the financial wherewithal to overcome it.

N

NUTRITION: HOT BUTTON #5 FOR THE MILLENNIUM

We all want to be healthy. We want to eat products that are good for us and avoid ones that may lead to disease or early death. What we say and what we do are, of course, entirely different. A large part of the problem, however, is confusion. Despite strict food-labeling laws and the efforts of consumer groups, the government, and manufacturers to educate consumers about nutrition, the public remains baffled by everything from advertising claims to the nutritional triangle promulgated by the U.S. Department of Health and Human Services.

We are cynical, too. The Nutritional Labeling and Education Act (NLEA) of 1990 regulates and standardizes what manufacturers can say about serving sizes or health claims and the use of descriptive terms such as "light" and "low fat." Still, we suspect that products that claim "less fat" may still have a lot more fat than we should be eating. And we're vaguely aware that "no cholesterol" does not mean "no fat," but we've also heard that not all cholesterol is bad for us. We've heard the same news about fat. Despite all this skepticism and confusion, we buy products that make health claims whether we fully understand them or not.

We feel better psychologically, even if the product does nothing to benefit us physically.

The NLEA regulations, which are enforced by the U.S. Food and Drug Administration, spawned a mini-industry of experts who spend their workdays determining what can and cannot be legally claimed on labels and in advertisements. It's important to realize that even the imperious government bureaucracy can be budged by compelling evidence that a product does, indeed, do good things for our bodies. After weighing the findings of numerous studies over the years, the FDA recently told oatmeal makers that they can make the claim that oat fiber helps reduce the risk of heart disease by lowering cholesterol.

Some health claims may not be worth making. It's one thing to get us to try a product once, it's quite another to convince us to repurchase it. I can't say this enough: It all comes down to taste. We've learned a thing or two as we've gone through various health-food fads over the years. One lesson is that "no salt" products definitely don't taste as good as comparable products that contain salt, no matter what flavors or additives the manufacturer substitutes. That's why you see far fewer "no salt" claims on packages today than you did a few years ago.

Whatever the health problems associated with salt, excess intake does not generally lead to consequences that other people can see, such as weight gain or acne. Eating too much sugar generally does. People who are worried about how they look are more apt to buy foods that make "low calorie" or "no sugar" claims, particularly now that artificial sweeteners taste better than they originally did.

Nutrition bars, which presumably provide a quick burst of healthy energy to athletes and road warriors alike, will continue to grow in popularity. We'll see a lot more vitamins and minerals added to products, as they are with cereals and some baked goods today. Phyto-nutrients (dietary supplements such as spinach tablets that contain plant constituents) and Nutraceuticals (enhanced food products with pharmaceutical or medicinal benefits) are another huge growth area. Odorless garlic tablets, which claim to increase circulation and to lower blood pressure and cholesterol, are also becoming a big business. And one of these days somebody will hit it big with a juice that combines the great taste of fruit juice with the nutritional value of vegetable juice. There are at least three brands trying hard right now, including Campbell's V-8 Splash.

I'm not suggesting that you rush out to build your own brand of nutrition bar or garlic tablet. Nutritional me-too products suffer the same problems as unhealthy ones. But think about what's making these products successful and apply those concepts to your own new-product development and marketing. No generation in history has been as concerned about its health as the Baby Boomers. As they ride into the sunset, you can bank on their continuing quest for foods, beverages, and services that purport to keep them fit.

NIX ON NEGATIVES

They say that a cliché becomes a cliché because it's true. One of marketing's oldest saws is that "Negatives don't sell." It's true.

Another old saying is "Horses sweat, men perspire, and women glow."

Revlon's No Sweat Anti-Perspirant managed to violate both of these adages. In effect, Revlon was asking women to purchase a product that prevented something that they didn't want to admit ever happened.

No Sweat came out about the same time as Degree antiperspirant, which is about as nondescriptive a brand name as a marketer could dream up. It's still being purchased, however. No Sweat might have been more aptly named No Sales.

Acknowledging consumers' negative feelings toward a product doesn't work either.

The idea behind I Hate Peas was that kids like French fries but hate vegetables. If peas, beets, and lima beans were disguised as French fries, kids would eat them. There's no group alive as blunt as kids, however, and they made their feelings clear. In one way or another, they said: "A pea is a pea is a pea. We don't like peas. In fact, we hate peas, and we won't eat them no matter how you disguise them."

And they didn't.

Remember that the next time you're tempted to name a toothpaste Avoid the Drill.

NEATNESS COUNTS

Invent a product that makes people's lives less messy and you'll succeed. Invent a product that requires wiping up after each use and you'll fail.

Toothpaste tubes have long been a source of unwelcome goo. Crest's Neat Squeeze toothpaste dispenser solved two problems that were only partially addressed by the pump containers that preceded it. It addressed the irrepressible human urge to squeeze the middle of the tube at the same time that it prevented paste from oozing out from everywhere. Chalk up a reason to buy Crest that has nothing to do with preventing cavities or gingivitis.

Dr. Care Toothpaste, on the other hand, was toothpaste for kids that was packaged in an aerosol can. You can imagine the results. Many parents did, and they didn't buy it.

Whatever you do, don't promote a product as being neat if it's exactly the opposite.

Pokems Neat Drink in a Bag from Ralston Purina caught many a parent's roving eye. Neat and drink are not words that moms and dads with young children usually associate with each other.

To drink Pokems, kids poked a plastic straw through a plastic bag that contained the beverage. They had to poke very, very carefully, however. At best, the juice leaked where the straw was inserted. At worst, it squirted or backed up through the straw. Observing this phenomenon inspired many kids to use the container as a water pistol. Some epic battles ensued. Pokems lost the war.

Think of a way to make your product easier to pour, simpler to dish out, or less messy to eat, and you'll have a significant point of difference that's hard to beat in a society that holds cleanliness next to godliness. Create a product that creates a mess and you'll be taken to the cleaners.

O

OOPS...

In the early 1980s the Campbell Soup Company introduced a line of pasta sauces under the brand name Prego. I sheepishly admit that I did not believe the market could bear another line of pasta sauces. Ragu was very popular. Aunt Millie's, Progresso, Hunt Wesson, and myriad other brands from regional packers were alternatives. Many restaurants with devoted followers bottled their own sauces, which were distributed in local supermarkets.

My first problem with Prego was the name. When I first saw it, I was reminded of Sophia Loren movies. I could almost hear the actress saying the word "prego," which I thought was a supplication meaning "please." And in English, "prego" sounded like "pray, go"—the sort of polite but urgent plea of a Shakespearean actor. Something like: "Pray go, Lothario, and tell Romeo that I do love him." More to the point, perhaps, "Pray go get thee a saucepan and dump the contents of this jar within."

I didn't—and still don't—think that a brand name should beg the consumer to do something. It's not quite as unseemly as the *National Lampoon* magazine cover that said "Buy this magazine or we'll shoot the dog," but a brand name should make a definitive statement, not a request. Anyway, that was my first mistake. Through its advertising, Campbell made the brand name synonymous with pleasing the palate. In retrospect, I think the name is quite good.

My second mistake was that I wrote about the product before I had tasted it. Prego was not just another version of Ragu. Its taste was vastly superior, with lots of spices and bits of tomato that gave it a consistency that seemed more like homemade sauces.

Campbell reportedly did its homework when it was developing the brand. It discovered that although Ragu sales were considerable, about 50 percent of Americans were making spaghetti sauce from scratch. Campbell set out to make a sauce that was so good that it could pass for homemade. The initial advertising campaign showed skeptical Italian families being won over by the bottled sauce. The tag line "It's in there" gained currency on its own as a catchphrase, and it's still remembered today.

Prego was so demonstrably better than anything else on the market, in fact, that Campbell ran into difficulty a few years later when it attempted to market Prego Plus. Prego already had a quality image in consumers' minds. They couldn't fathom why they should spend more money for a superpremium sauce that didn't taste significantly better. Prego Plus was the bomb that I thought Prego would be.

Hey, everybody makes mistakes. Even new-product experts.

ONCE UPON A TIME

Once upon a time, there were grocery stores in every neighborhood. Customers told the proprietor what they needed. He pulled it from the shelf and bundled it. The stores were small. Consumers had few choices. In most categories, the retailer carried only one or two brands. Shoppers often bought their fruits and vegetables at another shop, their meat at the butchers, their cod at the fish market. Although each proprietor was as responsive as possible to the needs of his customers, shopping was a slow, labor-intensive process. And there was little variety in the available goods from day to day.

Then the supermarkets came to town. They put many of the little stores out of business by offering the conveniences of one-stop shopping, increased variety, and cheaper prices. As time went on, the supermarkets got bigger and more plentiful. They were only minutes away from each other by automobile. Competition became fierce. Stores wooed customers by slashing prices. The profit on each sale was measured in pennies. Management explored other ways to increase volume.

One way to attract shoppers was to offer even more foods and brands to choose from. This encouraged manufacturers to develop new, better, and improved products. Brands grew strong and spread out across the land.

Another way to improve profits was to stock additional categories besides food items. Supermarket owners again added space to the stores and began to sell such items as toiletries and personal-care products.

Health-care items proliferated; stores opened their own pharmacies. Because the margins on nonfood items were so high, managers soon added other non-food merchandise. Gift merchandise. Cards. Magazines. Novelties that consumers might buy on impulse. Lawn chairs. Snow shovels. Toys.

Consumers could get even more of their weekly shopping done at the supermarkets, and distribution became more efficient for manufacturers as retail chains consolidated their assets and expanded their territories.

Consumers demanded more variety, and manufacturers responded with new flavors, sizes, forms, and brand extensions. Any new-product idea that came along was acted upon. If it sold, fine. If it didn't, the manufacturer went back to the drawing board and developed something else.

With so many products and brands competing against each other, the supermarkets realized that they controlled the manufacturers' access to the buying public. They began to turn the buying function into a profit center.

First, the supermarkets hemmed and hawed about whether or not they'd stock certain new products. Often, this was a tactical ruse. They really wanted heavy discounts on the wholesale price, or they expected manufacturers to issue coupons that would build traffic in their supermarket.

If the manufacturers did not cooperate, the retailers would delay or withhold the product. This led to uneven distribution. Marketers began to grow more cautious about what products they manufactured.

They only launched products that were familiar in concept (me-too products), or carried a familiar name (line extensions). Innovation plummeted.

The situation got worse.

Supermarkets began to stock new products only if manufacturers were willing to pay an up-front fee to gain access to their distribution systems. They called this a "slotting allowance." They summarily removed brands with small-but-loyal followings to make room for a procession of new, but seldom innovative, products that paid the slotting allowances. They pushed aside products that were just gaining a foothold.

They gave other products a short time to meet a sales quota. If they didn't, they had to pay another levy, which was dubbed a "failure fee."

Entrepreneurs with promising single-item products were unable to pay these exorbitant fees and were shut out of the process entirely. Sometimes they scraped together the slotting allowances, but then they had no money left to advertise and promote their product.

The supermarkets had forgotten why they were successful in the first place. They were no longer delivering to consumers the best variety at the best prices. They had become purveyors of shelf space. They were stocking the new products from which they could derive the highest profit. Consumers saw their choices narrow. Supermarkets not only cut out the superfluous sizes, shapes, and flavors that had proliferated, they also eliminated entire lines. In some stores and categories, there were only a couple of megabrands from which to choose.

As big and diversified as the supermarkets got, their bread and butter was still food. That's why people shopped in them. It takes expertise, after all, to handle and market perishable grocery items, and the supermarkets did it very well. On the other hand, it takes little expertise to handle the nonfood, nonperishable items that yield higher margins.

It came to pass that alternative store formats began to crop up. They came in several varieties and sizes and were known by different names. Mass merchandisers. Discount stores. Category killers. Warehouse stores. But they shared a modus operandi. They sold profitable, nonperishable items such as health- and beauty-care products at lower prices than the supermarkets did. This attracted consumers. The alternative retailers attracted manufacturers, too, not only because that's where the consumers were, but also because they did not demand up-front fees in order to stock new items.

Some supermarket-industry analysts were alarmed. They pointed out that supermarkets were losing sales in the general merchandise and health- and beauty-care categories. Supermarket management had learned some new jargon from MBAs, however. It replied that those products did not move all that fast in "number-of-turns-per-square-foot," anyway. They pointed to their bottom lines which, because of their fee-for-entry arrangements, were healthy.

Management decided that the stores themselves should develop a strong brand image so that they could be differentiated from one another. Each store began to stock its own brands with its own labels. These store brands did not have to pay slotting allowances, yet they occupied premium space on the shelves. They also sold for less money than the national brands that were saddled with high marketing expenses. Unlike store brands of the past, these products were top-quality items. They were also, in most cases, out-and-out knockoffs. Me-too products. They sometimes came in fancy packaging, but there was nary an ounce of innovation within their respective containers. And now that many supermarkets were stocking fewer brands, they decided that they could go back to building smaller stores, saving on real estate and construction costs.

The supermarkets thought they had it all figured out.

But as time went on, those alternative stores that had already snatched a share of the easy-to-handle products began to stock some of the more difficult-to-handle products. They built freezers and refrigerated display cases. They sold vegetables and fruit. They did not charge manufacturers exorbitant slotting fees for new products. Manufacturers began to ship products to them that were not made available to supermarkets.

All of a sudden, consumers not only perceived these alternative stores to be cheaper, they also began to think of them as convenient, one-stop shopping opportunities. They found a wide array of selections and product lines from which to choose. They could, in fact, buy anything from a snow blower to snow peas.

The conclusion of this tale is still up in the air as I write it in the late 1990s. The problem, however, is clear: Supermarkets are killing the geese that laid the golden eggs. The geese were the manufacturers who continually experimented to make innovative products; the golden eggs were the brands that resulted from the process.

Like so many other businesses that became obsessed with quarterly profit and loss statements and dividends in the 1980s, supermarkets lost the focus that had made them so successful in the first place: delivering what their customers wanted.

What customers want today is much different from just twenty years ago. Time is their most precious asset. They want to spend less time shopping and preparing food. They are experimenting with electronic ordering, but few supermarkets offer it. They are buying freshly prepared hot meals, which few supermarkets offer, at specialty markets. They think of the supermarket as a warehouse for necessities like laundry detergent and milk. They do not believe that supermarkets are interested in their needs.

Indeed, they are not. Supermarket profits depend on how much money they can extract from manufacturers. They are not focusing on how much choice and variety they can offer to their customers. Supermarket executives have become accountants and purchasing agents, not marketers. Pleasing customers has become secondary to pleasing shareholders. And the bards of the trade press have begun to write a new fable:

"Once upon a time, there were supermarkets in every neighborhood . . ."

ONLINE SHOPPING

Experts basically divide into two camps when discussing how people will shop for consumable products in the year 2000 and beyond.

One camp believes that online shopping will never be significant primarily because people enjoy the social experience of going to the store. They do believe that stores must become more fun to experience and should include all sorts of other services—from dry cleaning to banking—that were formerly separate destinations.

Seminar attendees at industry conferences like this viewpoint because it suggests that the shopping experience won't be much different than it has been. Just bigger and better. Stores that haven't expanded and added the fun factor yet will, of course, need the advice of outside experts to help them.

The other camp of experts is more optimistic about cyberspace. They believe that electronic shopping will capture somewhere between 10 and 20 percent of consumers' dollars within the next decade.

I think electronic shopping will capture as much as 30 percent of the market by 2005.

Time is our most precious asset, and we're learning to be penny-pinchers with it. We certainly don't want to squander it waiting in a checkout line.

A generation ago, futurists were predicting that we'd all have so much leisure time that we wouldn't know what to do with it. That obviously has not happened. People are working longer hours than they were. In most families, both spouses have jobs. Sometimes one parent comes home and the other goes off to work. There are more organized activities, from after-school programs for kids to charity walkathons, that require a commitment of time. The pace of everyday life is more frenetic.

The only people who truly enjoy shopping for the everyday essentials of life are people, as the teenagers put it, who need to get a life. Anything that makes shopping easier will prosper. I think that many people will begin to place regular orders for their groceries and perhaps go to the store once a month to check out what's new.

Online shopping has several inherent advantages:

- It's fast.
- Competitors are only a mouse-click away.
- Comparison shopping is easy.
- It eliminates middlemen, keeping prices low.
- Shelf space is virtually unlimited.
- Orders can be placed and delivered (or picked up, to save money) at any time of the day or night.
- There are no traffic jams, purse snatchers, car jackers, or bad weather.

Check back in a decade and we'll see how my prediction shakes out. (You might want to reread page 89, too. It's not for nothing that I bill myself as the New-Product Expert with an Historical Perspective instead of as a *Futurist Bearing Prognostications.*)

OFFICE POLITICS

You'd think that corporate America would be far beyond such parochial reasons for marketing a new product as "the boss likes the idea," or "the boss's husband likes the idea."

It's not.

But so what?

As long as people run companies, they will push their pet projects. That's not what I mean by office politics. In fact, many mid-level managers I know would be ecstatic to have a boss who took a firm stand on something. On anything.

I'm talking about products that are thrown into the marketplace without a chance of survival because of the politics of fear that dominate so many corporate hierarchies. Fear of failure. Fear of being blamed for failure. Fear of being perceived as fearful.

Here are some of the scenarios:

• *A bad concept continues to gather momentum because nobody has the guts to point out its flaws.* Somebody should have burst the balloon before Bird's Eye Soda Burst, an instant ice cream soda, got to market.

• *A project gets the green light because it "can" be done.* But everybody's afraid to ask the critical question of whether it "should" be done. The technology behind the Premier cigarette was amazing. But somebody should have stood up and said, "Just because we can produce a smokeless cigarette doesn't mean that we should. Who's gonna buy it?"

• *As silly as a concept may be, nobody wants to be accused of having missed an opportunity.* That's the type of thinking that results in flops like Legume Sweet and Sour Tofu with Ramen Noodles. It tried to appeal to too many constituencies. It failed to excite legume fans, ramen noodle fans, sweet and sour fans, or tofu fans.

• *A product rolls out because the executives associated with it are afraid to admit that they were too optimistic about its prospects.* In fact, they feel they must continue to hype it to their superiors to obtain a sufficient marketing budget. That marketing support will generate high initial sales. By the time sales drop because consumers don't like the product, the executives will have been promoted to another brand or recruited by another company. (Don't worry, I'm not going to name any names here. You know who you are.)

There's one other form of office politics that's sure to result in failure. Fear of taking responsibility. Someone has to take charge, make decisions, separate the good from the bad. Put an end to compromises that will weaken the product.

Someone once said that politics is the art of getting things done. That may be true. But when it comes to new products, office politics is the art of getting things dumb.

PICKET FENCES

The storybook American home has a front porch with a rocker. It sits on an ample plot of well-tended grass that's punctuated by a giant oak and surrounded by a picket fence.

That's a nice image, but most Americans live in entirely different settings.

For as long as I can remember, women and various ethnic groups have justifiably claimed that marketers develop products with little insight into how they really live and no understanding about their needs and wants. Products often have been created for women without a single female on the development team. Products have been targeted to black people without any input at all from African Americans. Although this seems to be changing, at least as far as women are concerned, marketers still develop too many products for themselves—and people like themselves—and not for the real people who are their potential customers.

Many senior marketers have MBAs or other advanced degrees. They work with other MBAs. They live in communities with people who have similar education levels and tastes. When they travel, they stay in hotel chains with rooms that are identical from Portland,

Oregon, to Portland, Maine. They eat in restaurant chains where the size of the New York sirloin varies by an ounce or two from town to town. The newscasters all look alike and talk alike wherever you are—indeed, who needs local news when you can watch CNN or read *USA Today*? I'm not finding fault. I'm just pointing out that our society is not quite as homogenized as we may think it is as we hop from one plane to another and try to keep a grip on our own professional and personal lives. The beaten path of airports and business hotels do not accurately reflect the richness of American culture, and our neighbors (or significant others) are often not our target customers.

In fact, too many new products seem to have been conceived or developed for spouses, neighbors, or business-school classmates rather than for real people in real situations. New products sometimes fail because marketers have never shared a beer with one of the members of the group they are targeting or used a product similar to the one they are selling.

Diversity is good business practice. Make sure your new-product team represents a broad cross section of America. But don't just rely on the input of others. Get out and meet people who are different from you. Read what they read, eat what they eat, buy what they buy.

And if you're going to market a new kitchen cleanser, don't be too proud to get down on your knees and scrub a few kitchen floors.

PACKAGING: HOT BUTTON #6 FOR THE MILLENNIUM

Packaging is as important to a brand as a cover is to a book, as a voice is to an actor, as a fit body is to an athlete. A fit body doesn't guarantee victory, but you don't see many potbellied Olympians.

Attractive packaging can turn even the most prosaic product into something special. Remember the store brands that became so popular during the 1970s and early 1980s? It was as if manufacturers were competing to make the chintziest packaging possible to prove that their products were true bargains. That has changed.

One of the primary reasons that private-label products are doing so well in the 1990s is because retailers have stopped making cheaply packaged imitations of the big brands. In many cases they've created such elegant packaging—from superior raw material to glitzy graphics—that some store brands have become serious competitors to the nationally advertised products. Stores now believe that a private label is one of the best ways to differentiate themselves from their competitors. If only Wegmans sells Wegmans-label products, consumers have to go there to get them.

Four trends should continue to drive package design well into the next century.

1. Special packaging, such as embossed labels, bottles embossed with logos, and special shapes and decorations, will continue to differentiate quality products from run-of-the-mill brands.

2. As me-too products proliferate, it will be particularly important to clearly communicate what your product is and what it does. And unless you're selling bubble gum or another product that only kids buy, MAKE SURE THAT YOU USE TYPE THAT AN OLDER PERSON CAN READ.

3. Less is more. Use as little packaging as possible

without making the product less easy to understand or use. This, of course, ties in with another Hot Button, the environment.

4. In a global economy, strive for the big idea. The shape of the Coke bottle, Pepsi's signature blue, and the Nike Swoosh logo translate well into any language.

PROOF OF THE PUDDING IS IN THE EATING, THE

Most people say, "The proof is in the pudding." Not true. It's a much more subjective judgment. What Cervantes actually wrote in his classic *Don Quixote* was, "The proof of the pudding is in the *eating* [emphasis added]."

If you've ever tasted sugar-free Jell-O Pudding, you know that's the indisputable truth. It's awful. That's not just my opinion. Most people agree, which is why sales are so poor.

"Healthy" foods that are tasteless are doomed to fail. On the other hand, there is no question that if you offer consumers a really sweet, rich-tasting product, you will have a winner. Häagen-Dazs ice cream—and all the superpremium competitors it spawned—has thrived during a time when many upscale consumers have moderated their eating habits. I know people who cut down on the main course so that they can indulge in a superpremium ice cream for dessert.

During my thirty years of collecting new products, there have been at least three surges for healthy, granola-type cereals. People say they want to eat healthy foods, and dozens of brands have competed for their business. The problem is that none of them have been very savory. They're tough to chew and, to palates raised on Cocoa Puffs and Frosted Flakes, flat to the taste. As much as consumers may speak about eating healthy, if something doesn't taste "right," they won't buy it.

Granola bars have been more successful as a category, but only because the product has been compromised so much. Starting with General Mills Nature Valley brand, mass-market granola bars have tasted more and more like a confectionery. But as chocolate and sugar crept into the category, the bars could hardly be considered healthy alternatives to Hershey bars and other conventional candy.

For years, manufacturers attempted to create snacks that health-conscious consumers could eat without feeling guilty. Dozens of low-salt or salt-free snacks and a slew of non-fried chips bearing the "no-fat" label have come and gone. So have many cookie and cracker brands. Some made "lower-fat" claims, others centered on a low- or no-sugar pitch. Some had an unusual initial taste; almost all had an awful aftertaste. Invariably, their significant point of difference from established brands was that they stinted on an ingredient that, in fact, made snacks taste good. The products' packaging and advertising usually amplified the negativity by shouting words like "LOW," "NO," or "NON." After years of tasting "no-fat" this and "low-sodium" that, consumers had come to the conclusion that the whole lot of them were "no good."

Nabisco finally got the formula right with its Snack-Well's line. The only difference between SnackWell's and the good-for-you cookies and crackers that came before it was that it tasted good. So good that the brand racked up more than $116 million in sales during its first five months.

The initial sales were as much testimony to Nabisco's distribution muscle and its clever advertising campaign as they were to superior taste, of course. (In the advertising, a "Cookie Man" character apologized to consumers because the company was unable, supposedly, to meet their demand for the product.) But SnackWell's, with three additional items, grew to half the size of the venerable Oreo business during its first full year, indicating that consumers really had been won over by the taste. It continues to expand today. Nabisco had a great brand name, lots of money, and the marketing muscle to make SnackWell's an instant success. But it would not have succeeded if it didn't taste better than most "healthy" food.

A brand with less marketing leverage but superior taste may also succeed in the marketplace, although it gets harder all the time without a major company to provide support. It took several years for Smartfoods cheese popcorn to gain recognition in the 1980s, but the company's attention to the quality of the popped corn and the taste of the cheese enabled it to expand throughout New England from its Boston base. It caught the eye of PepsiCo's Frito-Lay division, which purchased the brand and took it into national distribution. It still sets the pace for taste in its niche.

Frito-Lay more recently introduced Lay's Baked Chips, potato chips that are baked instead of fried. Frito-Lay virtually controls the chip business on a national level. The introduction commanded considerable promotion and attention. While it's far from being the first chip to claim little or no fat, it's the first to put "baked" in its name. Small competitors such as Guiltless Gourmet, Louise's, and No Fries welcomed the new Lay's Baked Chip because it would bring attention to the category. Most American's haven't yet tried the "healthier" version of a food they usually pig out on. Powerful as Frito-Lay is, if people don't conclude that Lay's Baked Chips taste as good as fried chips, it will fail. And probably take the category with it.

Distribution clout is important. A big ad budget helps immeasurably. A clever brand name is essential. But first and foremost, your food product must have superior taste. Put another way, you won't sell a thing if it ain't got that zing.

PREMEASURED PRODUCTS DON'T MEASURE UP

Although Americans love products that make life more convenient, premeasured products have never succeeded.

MaxPax Coffee, for example, was premeasured coffee packaged in filters that you simply dropped into the basket of your coffeemaker. It tested very well. It was easy to use, and the coffee grounds did not spill onto the counter or seep into the beverage itself. There was no way to adjust for the strength of MaxPax coffee, however, because the filters were sealed. Since coffee drinkers have widely divergent views on how strong a cup of coffee should be, MaxPax was destined to fail as a mass-market product.

Any product that restricts consumers' ability to adjust to circumstances runs a serious risk of failure, no matter how useful it may seem on the surface.

Soon after the Japanese conglomerate Kao purchased Jergens in the late 1980s, a few of its executives came to visit me at the New Products Showcase and Learning Center. They were intrigued by premeasured detergents that Amway and Colgate-Palmolive had recently thrown into wide distribution in the United States, evidently without benefit of a test. In addition, Procter & Gamble and Clorox were testing premeasured products of their own. Were premeasured detergents destined to be a twenty-first-century solution to harried consumers' laundry hassles? Could four preeminent soap companies be wrong?

First I brought out a box of detergent tablets called Salvo that had been marketed in the 1960s by Lever Brothers, the only major soap manufacturer that seemed to be sitting on the sidelines this time around. I explained the problems with Salvo, problems that some older shoppers probably recalled. (When you're marketing a new product, sometimes the biggest challenge is overcoming the bad impression that an earlier product left behind.)

The Salvo tablet didn't always totally disintegrate, often leaving a large glob of goo stuck in the folds of people's clothing. Further, as with MaxPax, consumers couldn't easily adjust the amount to be used. Sometimes consumers, particularly those with kids, need to use extra detergent. And if they have a load of delicate linens, they might want to use less. You could have hacksawed a tablet of Salvo in half or into quarters, but you would have negated the product's major benefit—convenience—the moment you did.

Then I showed the Kao executives samples of all the products currently on the market. The executions varied, but the concept was the same: less fuss, less muss.

In each box of Procter & Gamble's Tide Multi-Action Sheets—stick with me because this gets complicated, which is a problem right from the start—you got fourteen laundry "sheets" for $3.69. Each sheet contained twelve laminated, perforated pockets. Six contained detergent and six contained bleach. They were attached to a nonwoven backing. The powders dissolved in the water. When the wash was done, you placed the backing in the dryer with the load of clothes, and the heat transformed it into a fabric softener.

The problem was that people didn't always want to use bleach with their wash. Or fabric softener in their dryer. So they had to buy a separate box of detergent anyway to have on hand for those days when they didn't want bleach. And if they didn't care to use the fabric softener, they had to throw away the sheet after they finished the wash—an action that offends the frugal (see *Extraneous Extras*).

Clorox used a similar approach—with pouches instead of pockets—but it didn't compound the problem by adding bleach and fabric softener. Still, the basic issue remained: Consumers could not readily satisfy their urges to sometimes use more of, and sometimes use less of, the detergent. Again, once you start breaking into the pouches, the product loses its raison d'être. And nobody buys it again.

I could tell that the Kao executives' eyes were glazing over a bit as I ventured into raison d'être, so I circled back to the economic argument.

Many people buy big containers of detergent that

last for weeks and are good for many loads of laundry. Nobody's quite sure how many loads, but it seems to be a lot. And nobody—except, perhaps, a statistician in some federal bureaucracy—ever tries to figure out what the average load of laundry costs. But when you buy a box of premeasured anything, it's pretty tempting to divide the cost of the purchase by the number of uses you'll get out of it.

"Let's see, fourteen pouches. That's fourteen loads. Divided into three dollars and sixty-nine cents. Well, let's round that off to four dollars. Holy smokes! That's close to thirty cents a load!"

People felt that the price per wash seemed high. And guess what? It probably was high, since the manufacturer can't do all that extra measuring and packaging and shipping without charging for it. And even if consumers didn't do the price-per-unit calculations, they intuitively knew that they were buying the product more often than they usually did because the manufacturers simply cannot fit as much premeasured soap in pouches in a box as they can loose powder.

I can only assume that the Kao executives took my reservations to heart, saving millions of dollars in development and marketing costs, because I have not seen Kao market premeasured detergent either here or in Japan. For that matter, I don't see premeasured detergents on the shelves from Procter & Gamble, Clorox, Colgate-Palmolive, or Amway anymore either.

Consumers are aware that premeasured products have to be priced higher, and most don't want to pay the price. More important, perhaps, is that in many cases people value flexibility over convenience. Can you imagine the controversy that would erupt among cooks if someone were to attempt to premeasure "a pinch" of salt? The difference between a delectable meal and utter slop, a gourmet might contend, would be in the interpretation of that "pinch."

Q

QUESTION: WHO ARE OUR TARGET CUSTOMERS?

Many marketers ask: "What is our target market?" That's the wrong question. The one I always start with is: "Who are our target customers?"

When we talk about "the market" for a product we too often forget about human beings. We think in terms of "mass" and "niches." We measure success by our "share of market" or "slice of the pie." All these abstractions take us away from a simple truth: The market is people. Real people. I think it was David Ogilvy, the advertising genius, who suggested that marketers should not insult the intelligence of the consumer because she is their wife.

That's a bit quaint for today. To begin with, let's say that the consumer is our "significant other." The sentiment, however, is just as valid. When developing a new product you should always be thinking about the living, breathing, critical, credit card–bearing consumers to whom you expect to sell.

Your target customers are not some computer-generated overlay of Men of Scandinavian Heritage Who Like the Color Chartreuse with the latest census data and focus-group results. They are your uncle Harry, a truck driver who happens to be gay, and the woman who delivers the mail. They are individuals with whom you want to form a common bond. To do that, you've got to treat them like people, not like abstract pieces of data. You've got to develop a product that responds to their real needs, not one that simply reacts to a change in the marketplace. What do I mean by that? Let's look at the different approaches of two companies that sell paper towels.

When the Scott Paper Company started losing market share to cheaper, generic paper towels in the early 1980s, it responded with ScotTowels Junior—a product that only an engineer could love. Scott reasoned that if consumers could purchase a quality, branded product for the same price as the cheaper generic paper towels, they would. That's not a bad premise. But it proposed to deliver the quality product at a cheaper price by offering less product.

Rolls of ScotTowels Junior, which were 8.2 inches wide, were indeed chips off the old block. The normal paper towel roll was nearly 11 inches wide—the width that Scott itself had established as a standard more than three-quarters of a century before. Paper-towel holders with spring-like hinges at both ends could only hold 11-inch rolls. Scott was aware of this, of course, so it offered an adapter—a clear plastic pipe that was the width of the towel holders.

This approach had several problems. First, the adapters were shipped and displayed in a separate box, not packaged with the paper towels. Sometimes consumers didn't notice the box, or store clerks placed it too far away from the paper towels. Many consumers never gave a thought to the fact that the new product wouldn't fit their standard holders, and they didn't find out until they got the product home. Disappointed first-time buyers seldom give a product a second chance.

In time, Scott began to sell a paper-towel holder designed specifically for the ScotTowels Junior size. This was not popular either, except among the crowd whose idea of a good time is sinking screw anchors into kitchen walls on the weekend. And now Scott was not only changing the rules, it also was asking its customers to pay for it. If Scott was going to try to set a new (or alternative) standard, it should have given away the holders.

In short, ScotTowels Junior was a reaction to short-term market and economic factors, and not a response to the way that living, breathing people buy and use paper towels. In addition, Scott tried to make the case that ScotTowels Junior would "perform all of your regular towel jobs." That was a dangerous position for the company to take, however, because it suggested that its regular-size paper towels were an extravagance. Actually, it was creating a false problem to which it attached a bogus solution. It's mind-boggling to think of all the effort it put into trying to convince people that a product they'd used for decades was three inches too wide. ScotTowels Junior hung on for quite some time in selected markets, by the way, but never rolled out nationally.

In contrast, Procter & Gamble introduced Bounty Select-A-Size in 1994, a paper towel that also redefined a standard but did so in a way that responded to consumers' real concerns about squandering paper (and money).

Some people feel that they are wasting paper when

they use a towel for a small job, so P&G simply divided the standard length of a paper-towel sheet in half and added a perforation. Not only could consumers tear off a smaller sheet for little spills, they also could rip off a slightly larger one, if needed, for jobs that they thought deserved more than a single sheet but less than two. (Mothers have an amazing capacity to judge precisely how much toweling is required for a juice spill.) The width of Select-A-Size rolls was unchanged, however, and they still fit snugly into existing holders.

The major difference between Scott's and P&G's efforts underscores the difference between developing a product for consumers rather than for a market condition. Scott simply reacted to manufacturers that were undercutting it, while claiming a benefit that consumers recognized as false. P&G, on the other hand, responded to a real concern of its customers.

RUNNING HOT AND COLD

Where would we be without refrigeration and heating devices? We'd be in the nineteenth century, that's where. Food would be grown locally and be available only in season. Treats such as ice cream would be rare. It would take hours to properly prepare oatmeal, not the three minutes it now takes in the microwave. National brands would be limited to shelf-stable cans and bottles. It would be a very different world.

We sometimes take the ability to refrigerate and heat our food too much for granted, in fact, both as consumers and as marketers. Bad things happen when people take things for granted.

You're living dangerously if your product depends on machines like refrigerators, freezers, ovens, and microwaves to act in an ideal or uniform way. For example, it's a real challenge to bake an edible cake in a microwave by strictly following the directions printed on most boxes. That's because there's a broad difference in the power of microwave ovens.

And even if machines did work in a uniform way, consumers don't.

One new-product concept that leaves me scratching my head has been attempted by at least three manufacturers: microwaveable ice cream sundaes. Theoretically, the topping was heated in the microwave while the ice cream in the cup stayed cold and hard. But this was a radically different concept in food preparation. When was the last time you heated a product that was meant to be eaten cold?

Because the product was unfamiliar, and because it depended upon the correct use of both freezers and microwaves, microwave ice cream sundaes frequently ended up being mishandled at one—or several—of the following four locations:
- In the store
- On the way home
- In the purchaser's freezer
- In the microwave itself

Johnston, a Milwaukee sauce manufacturer, was the first to market a microwave sundae, which it called Hot Scoop Microwave Sundae. But Johnston had never made ice cream and wasn't well-versed in the intricacies of what can go wrong with refrigerated products after they leave the delivery truck. Its ice cream was packaged in small cups with little insulation. We've all seen piles of frozen goods waiting for clerks to place them in the supermarket's freezer case. Too many goods, too little time, and too little insulation equals a lot of mush.

Even if Hot Scoop survived the store, it faced an even more rigorous trial with consumers who dilly-dallied, made other stops, or got caught in traffic on the way home. The ice cream, as would any ice cream, went soft in the grocery bag. Then the consumer would put it in the home freezer. Most home freezers aren't kept cold enough to refreeze ice cream adequately, so that it was often softer than it should have been *before* it entered the microwave. Then the consumer would heat the sundae—and remember that microwave cookery is not an exact science and cooking times vary from oven to oven—only to pull out a cup of spongy ice cream covered with hot syrup.

Despite the problems that plagued Johnston, two experienced ice cream marketers, Steve's Ice Cream Company (Microwaveable Hot Fudge Sundae) and Weight Watchers (Hot Chocolate Fudge Sundae and Hot Caramel Fudge Sundae), tried their own versions of microwaveable ice cream. Perhaps they thought that their experience in the freezer case would produce a better result. Both attempted a different configuration of the cup itself. But neither firm addressed the fundamental problems in the way that the product is handled and the inability of most home freezers to re-freeze the ice cream to the degree that was necessary. They also failed.

Consumers concluded that the idea of microwaving ice cream was a poor one. They didn't realize that their actions (or those of store employees) caused the product to fail. They never do. And guess what? It's not their problem. It's yours.

ROYAL BLUSHES

If your brand eases people's embarrassment or self-consciousness about using a product, you're holding one of the strongest hands in the game of marketing.

When I shop, I'm nosy about what other shoppers are buying. Most other people are, too, whether they admit it or not. Because we recognize this, we bury items that we don't want prying eyes to see under other packages in our shopping carts. Still, there's no way—yet—to avoid the scrutiny of the checkout clerk, bagger, or the people standing behind us on line. That's why some products don't sell well in grocery stores.

No one thinks twice when he sees Pampers or Luvs disposable baby diapers in a shopping cart. We don't expect babies to be toilet trained. But people don't like to push around adult-incontinence pads. They buy them in drugstores or by mail instead. They worry that other people will wonder who in the family needs them (maybe the person pushing the cart). Recent advertising has attempted to remove the stigma attached to incontinence pads, and sales in grocery stores have picked up as a result.

Hemorrhoid relief is another example. For years, people overwhelmingly purchased the heavily advertised Preparation H. Yes, they were embarrassed, but the choice was pain or shame. Then products containing 0.5 percent hydrocortisone appeared that were not only effective in treating hemorrhoidal itching, but had additional uses such as relieving the itch of insect bites. These products cut into Preparation H's sales until it introduced its own version of hydrocortisone-based cream. The original Preparation H still does well, too, but the embarrassed buyer now has an alternative product that, as far as other nosy shoppers are concerned, could be for less private functions than relieving the discomfort of hemorrhoids.

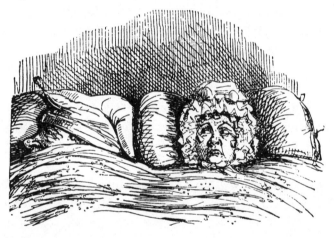

People get embarrassed about the strangest things. I recently heard a disc jockey pitch Dial-A-Mattress, a service that delivers directly to consumers. He talked about how embarrassing it was to go into a store to buy a mattress. He suggested that we worry that the salespeople wonder about what happened to our last mattress. Did we wear it out with some unspeakable activity? Is it pocked with unseemly stains?

We would not buy an easy chair without sitting in it or an automobile without driving it. Granted, some people just want to avoid the inconvenience of schlepping a mattress across town, but the Dial-A-Mattress sales pitch successfully plays to a totally irrational sense of shame.

Beano addresses a condition that has been mortifying people at least since the time of Chaucer, who describes a good soul of the fourteenth century as being "somdeel squaymous of fartyng." With the possible exception of first-graders and fraternity brothers, most of us remain "somewhat squeamish of breaking wind" in public today. That means that we sometimes pass up food that we'd like to eat. Beano contains a natural enzyme, alpha-galactosidase, that helps our digestive system break down the gas-causing sugars contained in some foods. It has become the fifth best-selling product in the antacid category even though it costs more than $5 for seventy-five servings and is produced by a small company without a lot of marketing clout.

Consumers will avoid products that may cause them embarrassment and will pay a premium for those that prevent it.

RATATOUILLE TO YOU, TOO, PAL

"Waste not, want not."

"Never throw out the dirty water 'til the clean comes in."

"A penny saved is a penny earned."

These precepts may seem quaint, but they have shaped the way that many Americans approach consumption. By nature, we're a thrifty people. Our attics and basements are testimony to our reluctance to throw away products that have long outlived their usefulness. We're not only reluctant to discard what we can no longer use, we're quite parsimonious about paying for things we don't need (see *Extraneous Extras*). It's only natural, then, that we absolutely refuse to pay for something we don't like. Funny how some marketers forget that.

Take TV dinners. In the early days of frozen meals, manufacturers discovered that the simplest meals were the best sellers. They packaged popular main courses such as fried chicken, complemented by mashed potatoes and a familiar vegetable. String beans, say, or peas. For dessert, they gave us apple pie. Bland, yes, but it was food that we all recognized.

TV dinners were considered déclassé, of course. And as time went on, the manufacturers wanted to entice more upscale buyers who were often similarly cosmopolitan in their tastes. They did this by adding a number of exotic vegetables to the platters. The problem was that kids wouldn't eat those vegetables. It was painful for us as parents to toss out "perfectly good food" when our heads were still reverberating with our own parents' evocations of "all those starving kids in China." So guess what? We didn't buy the product again. Why should we waste 25 or 33 percent of our investment in something that's a highly discretionary purchase? It was like paying full price for a carton of eggs only to discover that three or four are broken. Every time. After a while, we'd buy our eggs elsewhere.

Responding to consumers, manufacturers began to downplay their full-course dinner lines and, for a time, pushed frozen entrées without vegetables, potatoes, or a dessert. Then Campbell launched a savory new line of upscale frozen dinners with microwaveable—and reusable—sectional plates wrapped in attractive cartons. Full-course dinners became a booming business again. Competing brands positioned themselves as having less calories or less fat. About a half dozen me-too brands came out all across the price spectrum.

The result of all this, of course, was that manufacturers once again needed to distinguish their meals from their competitors' brands. And once again, instead of finding peas with your chopped steak or sliced turkey, you were just as likely to find ratatouille, squash, or okra. The problem was that these aren't the types of side dishes that Americans enjoy eating. Plain old green peas with gobs of butter are a hard enough sell in some households. Youngsters—and former youngsters—said "rats" to ratatouille.

What happened next? You guessed it. There was another massive consolidation in frozen products. Many of the exotic offerings, even entire lines, disappeared.

By all means, be innovative. But be realistic. You're not going to outsell your competitor's popular fried chicken and buttered peas dinner by introducing fried chicken with Brussels sprouts in strawberry vinaigrette. Being different purely for the sake of being different doesn't make the scanner hum.

REBATES DON'T PAY

As a consumer, I love rebates. As a marketing guru, I hate them. As a consumer, they allow me to pick and choose among several strong brands for the best deal. As a marketer, I know that every time I offer to shave my price, I'm undermining a hundred years of conditioning the American public to buy and trust specific brands for attributes other than their cost. That's not as cynical as it sounds. If the only thing that mattered was price, we'd all be dressed in army khakis and driving something as generically dull as the Chrysler K car (which was a dud).

The automobile market is a good example, in fact. Rebates became so common in the 1980s that most buyers started to wait until the cutthroat rebate season got into full gear before they'd even begin to shop for a new car. The same thing has happened in some packaged goods categories. There are so many coupons floating around that consumers began to think of the regular price of some products as a rip-off. They wouldn't buy a laundry detergent or a cereal unless they had a coupon. In an effort to recondition consumers, Procter & Gamble wisely instituted an "everyday low price" policy a few years ago. More recently, cereal marketers have slashed prices and curtailed couponing.

The world of rebates, price promotions, sweepstakes, and contests is filled with executional gaffes and blunders that could fill a book of their own. Don't even think about running a contest without bringing in a lawyer to make sure that you don't wind up wasting a lot of time in court. Even if you dot every legal *i*, it's a minefield out there. Always has been and always will be. And since we're on the subject, frozen dinners are an excellent case in point.

Swanson conceived the TV dinner in 1954 as a meal that could go straight from the freezer to the oven to laps parked in front of a television set. In fact, the TV was so much a part of the national consciousness at the time that Swanson's packaging mimicked a television set, with an image of the dinner displayed where the picture tube would be.

Although Swanson had been successfully marketing frozen meat potpies for three years, it was cautious about its prospects for this radically ambitious product. It only produced 5,000 units on its first run. The roll-out price was $1.09, but it was quickly knocked down to 99 cents. And the TV dinners sold like . . . well, like hotcakes.

The national roll out was supported by a huge ad campaign. That got Chuck Mittelstadt, a mentor of mine to whom this book is co-dedicated, into a big jam. Chuck was an executive with the advertising agency that handled the Swanson account. He devised a clever promotion to encourage consumers to try the new product: Buy one dinner and get a silver dollar in return.

Because everyone wanted to try these newfangled TV dinners that everyone else was talking about, they proved to be a great loss leader for the supermarkets. Discounts drove the retail price down to as low as 59 cents. So Chuck's deal amounted to Swanson paying consumers as much as 41 cents to eat its dinners. In those days, 41 cents would buy thirteen first-class postage stamps—the equivalent of $4.16 today.

The deal obviously was great for the consumer. And, ultimately, it was good for Chuck's client. Within a year, Americans scarfed down more than 10 million Swanson dinners, and TV dinners became a fixture in the freezer. But it wasn't so good for Chuck. As bril-

liant as he truly is, he temporarily found himself looking for new employment.

Moral of the story: There's no such thing as a free
dinner, either. Rebates may move product in the short
term, but in the long term, they don't pay.

S

SAVING THE RAIN FOREST (AND OTHER CAUSES DU JOUR)

Cause-related marketing became big business in the 1980s. Credit card companies affiliated with every niche group under the sun, and mutual funds that were politically correct in one way or another became popular in some circles.

I'm a firm believer in donating time and money to worthy causes. But don't sacrifice a good product idea to a cause du jour.

Don't get me wrong. It's smart for financial institutions to affiliate with college alumni associations and other nonprofit groups. It takes the edge off the annual charges that consumers pay. Even if the amount of money the institutions receive is minuscule, people feel good about it. They are less likely to jump ship for another credit card that's offering 2 percent less in interest charges. And some consumers like the idea of letting people know what causes they stand for, or where they went to school, by showing off the institutional logo whenever they reach for plastic.

But most products are very different from credit cards. Their value is in what they look like, taste like, or feel like. And their names and marketing programs should reflect those inherent benefits rather than external factors, like saving trees, feeding orphans, or promoting peace.

Ben and Jerry, the hippie-entrepreneur ice cream makers from Vermont, made liberal causes the center-piece of their marketing. Their Rain Forest Crunch flavor, for example, was supposed to raise people's consciousness about the destruction of tropical rain forests. A portion of the sales was donated to the cause of preserving them, and some of the nuts that were used in the ice cream were harvested from land that might otherwise have been cleared. But you know what really sold Ben & Jerry's ice cream, including the Rain Forest variety? Tasty, imaginative flavors. And a whole lot of butterfat.

Most cause-related efforts are silly gimmicks that simply don't work over the long haul. The parade of rain forest products in the early 1990s included Tropical

Rain Forest drinks by R.W. Knudsen with three unpronounceable flavors—Guanabana, Cupuassu, and Calamansi; Rain Forest cereal; Rain Forest snacks; and from Canada a Rain Forest cookie called Dare.

Wegmans, a supermarket chain in the East, introduced a private-label, two-flavor Tropical Rain Forest snack line. The cans contained such familiar treats as peanuts and dried fruit. Only a handful of nuts in each can were harvested from an actual rain forest. When I spoke to the manufacturer, I heard a long diatribe about how the product would make a big impact by raising people's consciousness about our vanishing rain forests.

It didn't though. Three Brazil nuts aren't going to save anybody's rain forest.

If you want to save the rain forest, write out a big check and put it in the hands of a reputable nonprofit organization. If you want to make the big profit that makes it possible to write out big checks, affiliate your product with benefits that are more universal, durable, and tangible than a cause du jour.

SCHEMES, STUNTS, AND MACHINATIONS

Whatever happened to the fine art of creating a stir for your product through wild and crazy schemes and stunts?

I'll tell you what happened. Press agents and copywriters became Media Relations Counselors and Executive Creative Directors. Boring executives who play it as safe as the rest of corporate America. Instead of hatching ideas to get your product's name in the news, they have underlings write tepid press releases that are indistinguishable from hundreds of others that go out on the PR Newswire. Or they spend gobs of your money for TV time and think their job is finished. Or they buy a two-second exposure of your mouthwash in a forgettable movie and think they've done something wildly creative.

The closest we come to the publicity stunts of yore is when some fashion czar stretches the boundaries of popular taste a bit further than the public will tolerate. Calvin Klein uses teens in provocative poses. Benetton creates purposely outrageous juxtapositions. The news media cover the controversy for a few days. But there's no lasting impact. People still talk about the series of Burma-Shave road signs that had clever jingles written on them, and they haven't been around since the early 1960s.

In the old days of hooey and hoopla, creative minds dreamed up schemes that changed the way we lived our lives. And they didn't have to resort to titillation to draw our attention (most of the time, at any rate).

Younger folks probably think that their right to a coffee break is written in the Bill of Rights. Not so. These pauses in the day's occupation were the result of a 1920s campaign by the N W Ayer & Son ad agency on behalf of an entity called the Joint Coffee Trade Publicity Committee.

"As regularly as the clock swings round to four, drink an appetizing, reviving cup of coffee," the newspaper ads urged the nation's workers.

The copywriter who dreamed up the campaign later professed that he feared "864,518 executives who are looking for the author with blood in their eyes and a determination to shoot on sight."*

In a nation filled with millions of coffee-drinking workers, he could well afford 864,518 enemies.

During the 1930s, when women were becoming a major market for cigarette makers, Lucky Strike came in tins. They were primarily forest green, with a red bull's-eye logo in the middle. The package had been heavily advertised and was readily recognizable. The trouble was that women didn't like it. They felt that forest green was a downright ugly color.

Because the president of American Tobacco refused to change the package, public-relations pioneer Edward L. Bernays set out to make green a fashionable color. Among other things, he concocted a charity event called the Green Ball. He attracted the cream of New York society to it. He also lured fashion editors to a "Green Fashions" luncheon where they heard an art historian and a psychologist expound on the glories of green. As a result, green became the rage of the 1934 fashion season.

Thinking like this could have saved any number of products that have failed in recent decades.

Back in the 1970s, Gerber discovered that a lot of college kids were snacking on jars of its baby food, for instance. Gerber executives reasoned that they'd get even more college-age consumers if they could ease people's self-consciousness about the product. Their solution: Offer labels to cover the famous logo of the cuddly Gerber baby.

---

* George Cecil is quoted in *The 100 Greatest Advertisements 1852–1958* by Julius Watkins (New York: Dover Publications, 1959).

What a boneheaded thing to do!

College students are notorious for their contrary behavior. They delight in flouting convention. Gerber was defensive when it should have been aggressive. It should have trumpeted the fact that college kids were eating baby food. It should have created events that made it a trendy thing to do. If clodhoppers like Doc Martens shoes can become fashionable, then Gerber's baby foods could have become a hip, outré, countercultural food to eat.

Kimberly-Clark's Avert Virucidal Tissues also could have benefited from big-picture thinking. First, words that end in *cidal*—homicidal, suicidal, patricidal—do not put people in a buying mood. And consumers had a hard time understanding what a "virucidal" tissue did. (It contained derivatives of Vitamin C that purportedly prevented germs from spreading by killing them when you blew into it.)

It's not that people are squeamish about killing germs, or even bigger bugs, as Raid commercials have demonstrated over the years. But they do like to know what they're slaughtering. I, for one, originally had only a general idea what kind of *viru* I was *ciding*. And until I knew for sure, I was just a little hesitant to sneeze into a tissue that kills it.

Clearly, people needed to be educated. And what better place to start than schools. The number-one customers for colds, after all, are schoolchildren. And teachers, even more than parents, dread infectious diseases.

Granted, people are at odds over the extent to which consumer products should be promoted in schools. Daily satellite-fed newscasts for high schools are contro-

versial because they contain commercials. But merchandising in our schools is nothing new.

Soap sales faltered in the 1920s because paved
roads and electricity were leaving people less grimy. An
ad hoc organization called the Cleanliness Institute
came to soap's rescue. It mounted a massive campaign
that included a "cleanliness curriculum" that dictated
standards for bathing and grooming at each grade
level.

Colgate used to give its Dental Cream toothpaste
to every schoolchild in America. Pamphlets that accompanied it promoted better oral hygiene and showed
the proper way to brush teeth. As a result, Colgate
Dental Cream was the leading family toothpaste for
years.

Kimberly-Clark had a similar opportunity. It should
have sent a big box of Avert to every classroom in
America and given tissue packs to every schoolchild to
take home, along with a pamphlet about colds and
their prevention. What teacher would argue against
distributing a tissue that kills cold germs? Imagine the
advertising possibilities of wholesome-looking kids,
happy teachers, and relieved parents clearly commu-
nicating the benefits of Avert. But first, Avert needed
to educate consumers about exactly what those benefits were.

Still skeptical about the value of roll-up-the-sleeves,
tub-thumping, get-the-people-talking-about-you stunts
and schemes? Do your marketing people tell you that
machinations and ruses are soon forgotten? That
they're only good for a quick sales jolt, not a sustain-
able buzz?

I'll tell you where you should tell them to go. On a coffee break, of course.

SIGNIFICANT POINT OF DIFFERENCE

A key principle of successful new-product marketing is to have a Significant Point of Difference from competing brands. If a Significant Point of Difference is not readily apparent (your product does not indisputably taste better, act faster, or clean more effectively), get it to the best advertising agency your money can buy. A good agency (see *Advertising Agencies*) will help you peel away all the layers of hopeful hype you've wrapped around your product and get to the heart of the matter—the one nugget you can really hype.

If you've got a winner, you've got a Significant Point of Difference. The Ted Bates agency used to call it the Unique Selling Proposition, or USP. And they came up with some doozies:

"M&M's melt in your mouth, not in your hand."

"Wonder Bread helps build strong bodies twelve ways."

These are indisputable points that probably would not have occurred to most people, but which rang a bell with consumers. The Wonder Bread new-product team certainly did not set out to create a bread that "builds strong bodies." In fact, I doubt that there was a new-product team. There was just another loaf of sliced white bread that needed to differentiate itself from the competition.

Note that neither of these claims crosses the line to deception. They were supported either by the consumer's experience (M&M's), or by the list of ingredients on the package label (Wonder Bread). Competitors were left flat-footed. How could you respond, after all, to M&M's' claim? "Our candy doesn't melt in your hand either"? The only way to respond is to create your own Significant Point of Difference.

It's particularly critical for a new product in a mature category to have a Significant Point of Difference. Consumers are generally comfortable with the same old brands and don't believe there's a lot of difference between them to begin with. Take bar soap, for instance.

For the most part, consumers feel that soap is essentially the same product, no matter what the wrapper says. We all know the names. Dove. Zest. Irish Spring. Camay. Dial. Lifebuoy. Safeguard. Ivory. Most of them fall into one of two camps. They either are deodorant soaps, which are favored by men, or they are moisturizing soaps, which are preferred by women. Dial is the best-selling deodorant; Dove is the top moisturizer.

When I was growing up, my mother always bought Sweetheart soap. I can't tell you why, but she was very loyal to it. Nowadays, however, consumers tend to pick the brand that's offering the best deal at the moment. "Special" sales are not so special because consumers have come to expect them (see *Rebates Don't Pay*). Price-cutting gimmicks like "get five bars for the price of four" dissolve brand loyalty. A shopper looking for a deodorant soap will buy Irish Spring instead of Dial at the drop of a nickel.

How could a new brand possibly expect to break into such a crowded, competitive marketplace and make money? By having a Significant Point of Difference. And by letting everybody know about it.

In 1991, Lever Brothers launched a new bar soap, Lever 2000, across the United States. Lever 2000 is a combination bar that offers the cleaning properties of soap, mild skin-care ingredients such as those in the Dove Beauty Bar, and a special ingredient, triclosan, that has deodorant properties. In short, it's a soap suitable for the whole family—dirty kids, sweaty dads, and moms with aging skin.

The soap was accompanied by a $25 million advertising campaign. The meaning of the futuristic-sounding (at least for a few years) "2000" was expanded by the commercials, which suggested that the soap was good for cleaning all 2,000 human body parts. Lever Brothers also got across the point that its new soap was different from all the others because it's effective for everybody in the family. One spot even showed a cuddly baby using it.

In its second year, Lever 2000 boosted its advertising budget to $40 million. It also launched an extensive sampling program, allowing millions of consumers to try the product. Consumers clearly related to Lever 2000's proposition that it combined all the individual benefits of soaps that had been favored by different members of the family.

There's another lesson in Lever's success. Most marketers nowadays try to capture a narrow sliver of the marketing pie by developing products that appeal to a particular demographic. Lever 2000 came on like gangbusters and proclaimed that it could be all things to all people. Its Significant Point of Difference was that it had something for everybody.

Don't get me wrong. I'm not saying that all you need to do to succeed is come up with a new product idea and then pay a lot of money to an advertising agency to produce commercials that proclaim you're different. The difference not only has to be significant, it also has to be real. If you're just another me-too product, you'll find yourself in an extremely costly battle with the established brands. And you'll probably lose.

The five-product Bayer Select line, for example, was launched with more than $100 million in marketing support in 1994. Bayer, of course, is well known as an aspirin. Four of the new Bayer products contained acetaminophen; one was ibuprofen-based. Acetaminophen and ibuprofen products had been cutting into aspirin's share of the painkilling market for quite some time. But the folly of Bayer's effort, beside the fact that it responded to a competitive threat a couple of decades too late, was evident on the label of Bayer Aspirin. Bayer Aspirin already claimed to relieve all of the ailments and pains that the individual Bayer Select products were purportedly addressing—headaches, menstrual cramps, sinus discomfort, and minor arthritis pain.

Bayer should have stuck to its knitting. Consumers didn't need another brand of acetaminophen and ibuprofen that didn't have a Significant Point of Difference from Tylenol, Nuprin, and all the other brands that have become entrenched on the shelves. Not only was Bayer Select a big flop, sales of Bayer Aspirin dropped 6 percent the year that Bayer Select rolled out, suggesting that the line cannibalized sales of the flagship product.

I should point out that Bayer, which has changed ownership, wisely refocused its marketing efforts on its aspirin. It's now heavily promoting its long-standing Significant Point of Difference as a "wonder drug." The Bayer Select line has receded into the shadows, and I'd be surprised to find it on the market at all in a few years.

SIZE: HOT BUTTON #7 FOR THE MILLENNIUM

One of my all-time-favorite brand modifications—the kind of creative thinking that could even give brand extensions a good name—was Ritz Bits. By miniaturizing its leading cracker, Nabisco gave it new positioning as a treat that could be eaten by the handful. Then they went a step further by adding cheese and peanut butter to form Ritz Bits sandwiches.

Marketing would be a snap if imitation alone ensured success. The Ritz innovation spawned many me-too experiments, but none came close to its success. Most of the copycat marketers weren't thinking about how consumers would benefit from the smaller size. Their motives had more to do with occupying more real estate: For the most part, subsequent products represented brand proliferation solely for the sake of more shelf facings.

Making your product smaller isn't the only direction to go in, of course.

Just as Pepsi was "twice as much" as Coke in the 1930s, Arizona Iced Tea's 20-ounce cans and bottles were deliberately larger than Snapple's in order to make a splash. Larger size packages are also prevalent at club and warehouse stores such as Sam's and

Costco. Consumers automatically equate bigger size packages with a bargain, even though the cost-per-ounce is sometimes higher than the normal size packages in a supermarket. I think that consumers will catch on to this soon, and bigger packages will truly have to deliver value.

Vary and fluctuate size—whether it's the package or the product within—to extend the positioning of existing products and to differentiate new ones from competitors'.

SOME THINGS OLD CAN BE NEW AGAIN

If a brand is flat or declining, find out what made it popular in the first place. Mature brands often have gone through several repositionings or reformulations. Sometimes these tweaks were terrible mistakes. Sometimes they were right for the time but no longer apply. Often a very powerful selling point has been lost or even purposely jettisoned. Never waste precious new-product development funds when you can revive a proven winner.

For example, Alka-Seltzer ought to get a Flop, Flop, Fizzle, Fizzle Award for all of its misbegotten extensions into capsules, caplets, and coated pills that are just like everybody else's capsules, caplets, and coated pills. Worse yet, it's sitting on a brand that could be revivified.

When *Advertising Age* named the Fifty Best Advertising Campaigns produced during the first fifty years of television, Alka-Seltzer was among the most prominent brands named. The magazine chose only four campaigns to represent the entire decade of the 1950s.

Alka-Seltzer commercials starring Speedy, the animated tablet that did a song and dance routine, was one of them. The brand's vignette-style advertising in the 1960s and 1970s that was most memorably represented by the "Mama Mia, atsa some spicy meatball" and "I can't believe I ate the whole thing" commercials was cited as a "hall of fame unto itself." And then, *Advertising Age* pointed out, Speedy returned once again with a catchy, new "Plop, Plop, Fizz, Fizz/Oh what a relief it is" jingle.

Alka-Seltzer told a simple, graphic story: Plop, plop. Fizz, fizz. Tablets dissolve. Fast relief.

It also was a unique story. The only real competitor, Bromo-Seltzer, fizzled away long ago.

But in the 1980s, Alka-Seltzer went the way of Tylenol and Bayer and many other internal analgesic manufacturers and started pushing conventional pills for a variety of ailments. That was a huge mistake. There's no visual pizzazz to gulping down a caplet. There's no action for consumers to see and believe.

Once Alka-Seltzer became a copycat, it became an also-ran. I went to the store to buy some tablets recently and couldn't find any. Indeed, why should retailers stock it? The tablet's unique benefits aren't supported by its advertising. In the minds of consumers, Alka-Seltzer is just like everything else. Bring back its effervescent personality and I bet sales will surge once more.

Similarly, Philip Morris's Miller Brewing Company spent millions of dollars developing and launching Clear Miller Beer when the clear-product frenzy was sweeping the nation (see *Fooling with Your Cash Cow*) in the early 1990s.

Clear Miller Beer didn't look like a real beer, and perception is an important part of the gustatory experience. Drinking Clear Miller was like drinking Möet & Chandon from a recycled Welch's Jelly jar. It just didn't seem to taste right. Miller quickly pulled it from distribution after it bombed in test markets.

Why didn't Miller spend the money it wasted in developing Clear Miller from scratch on resurrecting Miller High Life, a once-popular brand that has suffered a market share free-fall? All it needed was a straightforward advertising campaign that talked about Miller's long-standing attributes.

For years, Miller High Life was the only beer on the market that was bottled in clear glass. I can almost see the advertising: "Clearly Purer." "The Brand So Pure You Can See It." "We've Got Nothing to Hide." Any tag line that got across the idea that Miller High Life was purer than the competition, which hid their murky coloring behind green or brown bottles, would have served the dual purpose of conserving R&D funds and reviving a venerable brand.

SEER SUCKERS

Some marketers only listen to consultants who pat them on the back and tell them how brilliant they are.

And some consultants are brilliant at listening to what their clients say and feeding it back to them with flowery words and costly invoices.

Don't be a Seer Sucker. Seer Suckers pay consultants lots of money just to hear that the future for their proposed new product is as rosy as they hoped. Seer Suckers shut their ears to anything negative.

A few years ago, a businessman sought my opinion about how to market a baked, crispy, potato-chip-like snack product that he had just purchased the rights to sell in a region of the United States.

The package was a paper bag with a cellophane window through which I could see the chips. They were very heavily sprinkled with powdered sugar. When the chips moved around in the bag, they set up a charge of static electricity on the cellophane window. As a result, the powdered sugar clung to it like snow on a windshield. It looked very unappetizing, unless you were in the mood for a heaping dose of confectioners' sugar. Furthermore, when I ate the chips, the sugar spilled all over my chest and lap and left my hands a sticky mess.

I thought the businessman had purchased the rights to a loser. I advised him to avoid wasting a lot more money trying to bring it to market without insisting upon some modifications. This is not what he wanted to hear. He thought I was finding faults that normal consumers would not see or feel.

Right about the time that our meeting was getting a bit testy, my wife and office manager, Jean, dropped into the conference room to ask me something. Without betraying my feelings about the product, I asked for her opinion. It was as if there had been a hidden microphone in the room and Jean had been listening to my earlier complaints. As powder dribbled down the front of her blouse, she repeated my critique almost verbatim.

That's when the businessman stood up. His associates quickly followed. He announced that he was going ahead with the launch anyway and stormed out of the office, entourage indignantly in tow. To this day, I can't help but wonder how much money he squandered because he refused to pay attention to some commonsense advice that he had paid us good money to give.

If you think highly enough of a consultant to pay for his advice, listen to him closely whether or not the message is one you want to hear. That's not to say that consultants are always right. If they were, they probably wouldn't be consulting, they'd be early-retired moguls. But don't discard what they tell you simply because it's not what you want to hear. The best advice is often the hardest to swallow.

SUGAR DADDIES

I am a diabetic. I also love pancakes smothered in maple syrup. That, dear reader, is a classic dilemma.

Most sugar-free syrups made for dieting or diabetic consumers are little better than maple-flavored water in both taste and consistency. Every syrup I ever tried was immediately sucked up by the pancakes, leaving them an unappetizing mass of soggy dough.

Then one fine day in 1989, while strolling the aisles of the Fancy Food Show, I came across Betty Jo Steel and her line of sauces made with an artificial sweetening ingredient, lycasin, that nutritionists say is safe for diabetics to ingest. Her sugar-free Old-Fashioned Fudge Sauce and White Fudge Sauce with Toasted Almond were absolutely delicious. So, too, were some fruit-based sauces that tasted like the real thing. Alas, she did not make a maple syrup.

Over time, I became friendly enough with Betty Jo to suggest that diabetics would love to have a sugar-free maple syrup that would be worth pouring over their pancakes. Betty Jo and the supplier of her sweetener went into development mode. A few months later, I was presented with one of the first bottles of Steel's Country Syrup Sugar-Free Real Maple Flavor. As I burrowed into a mound of syrupy pancakes, the thought occurred to me that the 8-ounce bottle in front of me was one of the most satisfying consulting fees I'd ever earned. That may have been a bit of a rationalization. I normally work for a lot more than my breakfast, but I knew that was all Betty Jo could afford to pay me at the time.

Steel's Country Syrup is a product that even non-diabetic consumers would enjoy because it is thick, tasty, and virtually indistinguishable from sugar-laden syrups. Unfortunately, most people are not aware of its existence. Like many other products, it languishes in obscurity for want of a fraction of the marketing budget that the major food companies throw behind even the most minor line extension. Steel's Country Syrup is precisely the type of innovative product that is being murdered by the exorbitant slotting fees that supermarkets charge.

Fortunately, Betty Jo has been able to persevere because her husband is an accomplished surgeon and her livelihood has not depended upon nonexistent profits. Although she tells me that a decade of hard work is about to pay off, if Betty Jo's husband had been an average Joe she would not have been able to keep her business running long enough to reap the rewards. And diabetics would have been deprived of an excellent line of sauces.

I've thought long and hard about the problems that small start-ups like Steel's face in a world that is increasingly dominated by companies with deep pockets. It's everybody's loss when products that truly fill a need wither away for lack of financial support or distribution clout. Solutions evaded me until I read about a "greenhouse" program that America Online initiated. It supports entrepreneurs who have ideas for content that would appeal to its subscribers. If America Online approves an entrepreneur's proposal, it provides funding to get the project off the ground. It also gives the entrepreneur an established channel of distribution to more than eight million potential users. In return, it takes a piece of the action.

This is a win-win-win situation. The entrepreneur gets start-up capital, guidance, and distribution from the world's largest online service. America Online gets proprietary information or entertainment that enhances its reputation as a premier content-provider in cyberspace. America Online's users get access to innovative programming. Cyberspace itself is richer for content that might otherwise have died aborning.

The Procter & Gambles, Philip Morrises, and RJR Nabiscos of the world would be wise to study the America Online idea and develop greenhouse programs of their own.

SWIMMING AGAINST THE TIDE

There is an ebb and flow to the marketplace. If you don't know how to read the tide, it's easy to get caught in the undertow.

Kraft's Chicken Applause line came to market just as microwave ovens were becoming popular. Although consumers later learned that some foods are just not meant to be nuked by microwaves (see *Technology for the Sake of Technology*), at the time they were wild about the potential of this quicker, easier way to prepare meals. Unfortunately, Chicken Applause did not provide microwave directions. In fact, the packaged mixes (to which chicken was added) went right up against the prevailing tide toward simplicity. They required several steps to make a decent dinner, which took as long as one hour and fifteen minutes in some cases. Few cooks were willing to go through all that rigmarole, and few families were willing to wait more than an hour for a dinner made from a prepackaged mix. Chicken Applause, which might have been a hit before the microwave appeared (and at a time when there were more full-time homemakers with the time to prepare elaborate meals), was a bomb in the 1980s.

You can't swim in water that's too shallow, either.

Constant Comment, a premium brand of hot spiced tea manufactured by Bigelow, was ahead of its time when it decided to make a ready-to-drink version with a sparkling base a few years ago. Americans do like their soft drinks to sparkle. But effervescent iced tea was just too much of a stretch for the buyers at major supermarket chains on the West Coast, where Constant Comment Sparkling Iced Tea was supposed to test. Most of the buyers refused to stock it, and few consumers ever got a taste of it. Things might be different today. Some effervescent coffee sodas have at least gotten a trial, and the New Age category has certainly proven that anything goes with beverages.

Finally, more than a decade ago Baker Tom's was touted as "the only baked cat food." Consumers didn't know how cat food was made, however, and they didn't really care. Nobody equated "baked" with "better for my cat." At least they didn't back then. There's so much talk today about snacks that are "baked, not fried" that it's possible cat lovers would sweep Baker Tom's off the shelf if it were tried again—although it also would have to be a bit more chewable than the last version was.

A cat may have nine lives, but unfortunately, a new cat food doesn't. There aren't many opportunities for even a second chance, in fact. If your new product is swept out to sea or founders on the shoals because you've misread the tides and currents, consider yourself the captain of a shipwreck.

SHOCK VALUE

As a rule, I prefer substance over style. I have to admit, however, that a little showmanship or packaging pizzazz can go a long way. It seems that almost anything goes these days, in fact, as long as it jolts people out of their complacency.

For more than a dozen years I've been drawn to an exhibitor at specialty-food trade shows who calls himself Uncle Dave. He dresses in Farmer John denim overalls, flannel shirts, and a bright red woodsman's cap. You wouldn't give Uncle Dave a second thought if you saw him gabbing away in a general store in Vermont, which is where he hails from. But at trade shows, where vendors are usually dressed conservatively, he stands out like a maple tree in all its blazing autumnal splendor. You can't miss him if you look down the aisle.

As unusual as his appearance is, though, Uncle

Dave is down-to-earth, friendly, and usually engages in a couple of conversations at the same time. I'm always eager to chat with him myself. Just like his products, Uncle Dave is all-natural, with a touch of spice. It helps, of course, that his salsas, sauces, mustards, and so on are top-notch products—don't miss the horse-radish sauce with shredded carrots—and that he's always coming up with something new to exhibit.

The labels on Uncle Dave's condiments feature a caricature of him, replete in overalls and red cap, literally reflecting his homespun personality and appearance. The jars are as successful at catching a passerby's eyes as the heavyset, bespectacled entrepreneur is in the flesh. In the end, that's more important to supermarket buyers who attend the trade shows than the way that Uncle Dave appeals to them personally.

I admire the distinctive packaging for the Arizona Iced Tea Company, too. The original, unusual size and shape of the bottles and the Southwestern motifs of the labels not only stand out on the shelf, they also exude a sense of quality. Newer versions continue to cut through the clutter. The Indian's head on its Piña Colada label looks as if it has been silk-screened; there's a pretty, delicate print on the label for Green Tea with Ginseng. These packages almost demand that you pick them up for closer inspection.

And I have to admit that even packaging that I personally find to be atrocious has been successful in making an impression on shoppers' glazed-over eyes. For example, I initially gave the Inner Beauty Company's line of Blue Marlin fish and assorted hot sauces about a one in five chance of success solely because of its trashy appearance. The bottles are reminiscent of the pint-size whiskey bottles that derelicts seem to favor. The labels are crude drawings of ugly masks that have a Caribbean island look about them, although the sauces are made in Costa Rica. In retrospect, I was wrong. Because the garish design commands attention—and the sauces themselves are good—the line has gained widespread distribution.

And I've got to begrudgingly tip my cap to some products whose names I would have thought too vulgar for kitchen products a few years ago. I wouldn't put Ass Kickin' Cajun Hot Sauce on the picnic table if I were charbroiling some chicken wings for our minister, but there's a rough-and-tumble charm to this brand's label that hits home with people who are tired of gushy names along the lines of Ye Olde Bar-B-Que sauce. Another colorful line is the Bone Sucking Sauce collection of marinades for meat and fish.

The ways things are going, I wouldn't be surprised to see a Burp brand of beer with a picture of an ample-bellied couch potato on the label. And why not? If you've got it, as the saying goes, flaunt it.

SHOULD I OR SHOULDN'T I?

Am I or aren't I? Do I or don't I? Can I or can't I?

Your product should be answering questions, not forcing your customers into an internal debate with themselves. They are already overwhelmed by all the decisions they have to make in their business and personal lives. They don't want to be confronted by products that demand that they make more choices. Country People/City People Shampoos did just that.

Everyone agrees that there's a big difference between the quality of life in the city and in the country. The only debate is over which way of life is better. The marketers of Country People/City People obviously felt that, without taking sides, they could exploit this dichotomy that everyone agrees on. They designed two almost identical plastic bottles, one black and one brown, with an explanation on the package about the special formulas contained within.

The problem was that to make the concept really clear, the products had to appear next to each other on shelves. The City version obviously didn't sell well in stores that were deep in the hinterlands. And the Country version was a flop in cities. Many stores had an inventory of 50 percent of their investment sitting on their shelves. Store buyers weren't inclined to restock when half the order wasn't moving.

But the problem was even worse in the suburbs, where the decision could conceivably go either way.

"Let's see, there's a beautiful town park down the road a piece where the farmer's market is run on Saturdays," someone living in Fairfield County, Connecticut, might think to herself. "So I guess I'm a country girl. Hmmmmm. On the other hand, I'm on the 7:01 out of Greenwich to midtown Manhattan five days a week. I wonder which one is right for me?"

If you force consumers into an internal debate, the answer, nine times out of ten, is going to be a different brand entirely. A product should answer questions, not pose them. And if you've got the answer, let the world know about it.

Some manufacturers are shipping new products in special display cases that stand in the aisle and call attention to the product. They have to pay more for the real estate, of course, but it's worth it if it's done right. Procter & Gamble, for example, created a tiered plastic stand for its FIT Produce Wash. There's room for a regular-size plastic bottle with a sprayer on top, as well as for a refill jug. When the display was placed in the produce department in test markets, FIT sold briskly. It offered an answer to a problem that's on many consumers' minds: How can we be sure that there's no chemical residue on the fruits and vegetables we buy?

The eye-catching display also suggested the question to other consumers who may not have thought about it, which got the product into trouble at some supermarkets. Managers felt that FIT made consumers unduly wary about the cleanliness of their produce. They responded by stocking FIT in a different location in the supermarket. Sales dropped drastically, even with major advertising support. Away from the fruits and veggies, FIT is out of context. It's like responding "George Washington was our first president" to the question "Who won the World Series?"

Unfortunately, just as you don't get any points for correctly answering the wrong question in school, you don't make a lot of sales by doing something similar in the real world.

T

THOU SHALT NOT DECEIVE

This must be one of your cardinal rules. Nothing makes me angrier than to unwrap a product and find that it's less than the promise contained in the illustration, name, or advertising.

I've written that you should emphasize the positive and obfuscate the negative. Certainly, you must always put the best face on any product. But it's a terrible mistake to deceive the consumer by promising something that you can't, or won't, deliver.

Yes, I'm drawing a fine line. But it's easy to determine when you've crossed it. Forget for a moment that you earn your living as a professional marketer. Think about some of the things that make you angry when you're Mr. or Ms. Average Consumer with a mortgage, taxes, and rebellious children to worry about. Then check to see if you are guilty of any similar transgressions in your marketing. It's as simple as that.

Just last night, for example, a picture of sumptuous chicken bits and wild rice had my mouth watering for a frozen dinner that was described as "hearty" and containing "50 percent more." When I sat down to eat the meal, I found myself staring at six measly pieces of chicken, a splash of gravy, and hardly more than a dollop of wild rice. I cannot imagine what the original meal was like if this version was 50 percent heartier, but you can be sure that I will never buy a product from that line again.

Sometimes an entire category seems infected with deception. Consider frozen pizzas. The illustration on the box usually shows a luscious pizza with lots of bubbling cheese and generous toppings. But when you open the package, you find a sprinkling of cheese and paltry toppings. I now buy pizza at the supermarket only if it's wrapped in cellophane. I don't trust any pizza in a box.

And how about salty snacks? We're all aware that snacks "settle." But the bags of some brands are inflated like a beach ball. Burst the bubble and you discover that they're half empty before you've eaten your first chip.

Deception isn't limited to food items.

Most hair conditioners, dandruff shampoos, and combination shampoo/conditioners don't work half as well on mere mortals as they do on the actors in advertisements. The dandruff comes right back, or your hair won't comb well. My wife can never duplicate the sheen she sees on the models' hair in *Woman's Day* advertisements. And I can't understand why shampoos for kids deliver tangle-free tresses while some adult versions leave you pulling out tufts of hair. No wonder the market is always flooded with new shampoos. Why can't any of them perform the way they do on television?

In the same vein, I can't understand how we could develop a technology that allows astronauts to dangle from tethers in outer space while my rearview mirror consistently falls off the windshield of my car for no apparent reason. And why in the name of $100 screwdrivers does it cost $18 to reglue it? Again and again. My mechanic says this is inevitable for my model of car. That's outrageous. In fact, nearly every month brings an unforeseen problem with my automobile. The radio-controlled lock system suddenly won't operate; the hand-brake warning light won't shut off; the right-hand door lock won't go down; the grid protecting the catalytic converter falls off; the radio antenna jams. Sure, the car looks like the sleek machine in the slick advertisements I've seen, but it sure doesn't behave the way I was led to believe it would. I think of it as a pricey bucket of bolts. Think I'll buy another one? You'll catch me in an Edsel first.

My dander is really up now. But I bet you'll get on a roll, too, if you start thinking about some of the products you've purchased that haven't delivered on their promises. That have burned you. And that's my point. You know you've crossed the fine line between being positive and being deceptive in your claims when your customers are able to spew out complaint after complaint as if they are sworn enemies on a mission to destroy you.

A study I saw claimed that it takes about seven times the effort to win back disgruntled consumers than it did to acquire them the first time. That's a generous estimate from my perspective. Once you've burned me, you're history. Like most of your customers, I take your promises—direct or implied—very personally.

It takes an enormous amount of money (about $50

million for a new shampoo; perhaps $20 million for a pet food) to build a new product into a major, viable brand. Unless you intend to keep the promises you make, you might as well give that money to one of those well-tethered astronauts to let loose in outer space.

TECHNOLOGY FOR THE SAKE OF TECHNOLOGY

The items I see most often at garage sales, besides "like-new" Stairmasters and exercise bikes, are bizarre cooking devices. Fondue makers. Bread makers. Popcorn poppers. Electric carving knives. Waterless pots. The sort of gadgets that you see advertised on television at 4 A.M. that sound great but turn out to be more trouble than they're worth.

Consumers always judge the claims of new technology against the traditional way they've done things. Unless it offers a concrete benefit—it eases preparation or cuts down on cooking time, for example—they will stick with the tried-and-true.

The microwave oven has been a major new-product success story. Nearly 90 percent of American households now own one. It's very useful for boiling water or for warming-up leftovers. But it's not as useful as many people thought it would be. And it's not as versatile as a lot of product marketers hoped it would be. In the long run, consumers will reject a product that's specifically developed for new technology like the microwave unless it tastes better or cooks quicker than existing products.

We experienced microwave hysteria during the late 1980s and early 1990s. Every product, it seemed, had "microwaveable" scrawled across its packaging, and microwave cookbooks flooded the stores.

During this time, Hershey Foods introduced Perfection Microwave Pasta and Borden launched a line of microwaveable pasta under its major brand name, Creamettes. Both lines were regular, run-of-the-mill pasta. There were no accompanying sauces. No health claims. Nothing to differentiate them from the pasta that consumers were already buying except that they were microwaveable. In fact, that's all they appeared to be. Neither product offered label directions for preparing the pasta normally in a pot of boiling water. Could the pasta be cooked the usual way if the microwave was being used for something else? Consumers weren't sure.

Most troubling, there was no clear advantage to microwave preparation. Because of power variations among microwaves, chefs weren't sure how long to cook the microwaveable pasta. It was easy to undercook. Or—far worse—to overcook, which resulted in a dish of mush. It's much easier to sample pasta in a pot of water to make sure it is done. And if these microwaveable pastas offered any savings in preparation time, it was minimal.

In short, the microwave pastas weren't any better than regular pasta. They weren't tastier. They did not have a superior consistency. They weren't easier to prepare.

Microwave popcorn, on the other hand, has been a runaway hit because it's easier to make than traditional popcorn. Perhaps more important, it's easier in the aftermath, too, since the popcorn pops in its own container and there are no oil-soaked pots or (expensive) electric gadgets to clean. Popping popcorn on the top of the stove was exciting (see *Fun: Hot Button #4 for the Millennium*), but it sure could be messy.

If you expect to change the traditional way that consumers prepare something, particularly if it's relatively easy to begin with, your product must offer a genuine advantage over existing brands.

WHAT'S IN A NAME?

Well, not to pick an argument with Shakespeare, but that which we call a Häagen-Dazs might not, by any other name, taste quite as sweet.

Häagen-Dazs is a snooty-sounding combination of meaningless words that lends a certain cachet to an ice cream brand that was first made in New Jersey by a native of Brooklyn. When Häagen-Dazs created the superpremium ice cream category in the 1960s, there certainly were any number of local ice creams that were just as rich in fat (and arguably just as tasty), but none were sold nationally for as high a price. The name suggested that the brand was imported, and foreign products are often viewed as superior.

Ironically, the brand is now being sold overseas as "America's Number One Luxury Ice Cream," and is currently owned by the British conglomerate, Metropolitan PLC. The fact that "Häagen-Dazs" doesn't mean anything in any language doesn't matter because it avoids a big mistake many people make in naming products. Häagen-Dazs is both pronounceable and memorable.

You can be pronounceable and memorable but also be dumb, of course.

I still haven't figured out Clairol's Look of Buttermilk Shampoo, which was tested in south Florida for about three years. Most of my associations with buttermilk have been unpleasant. It is thick, gooey, sometimes lumpy, and often foul-smelling. For what earthly reason would anyone want such a substance in her hair? And what has "look of" got to do with buttermilk? The look of lumpy? Greasy? Tangled? I suspect Clairol meant to impart "fresh." But what is "fresh" hair? No one I've ever spoken to, at Clairol or elsewhere, has been able to tell me.

Clairol also tried a Touch of Yogurt Shampoo about

the time that yogurt was catching on as a healthy snack. The concept of slimy yogurt in the hair seems little better than buttermilk. There's a marketing adage that you should sell the sizzle, not the steak. A Touch of Elegance *with* Yogurt might have worked better because yogurt was considered good for you, but Clairol unsuccessfully tried to sell the steak.

Some names defeat themselves.

Lysol Laundry Sanitizer, which has been restaged or repackaged at least four times, is still on the market, although I can find no one who really understands what it is or can adequately explain the big problem that the product purports to solve.

We expect that we're getting our clothes clean when we wash them with our usual detergent, and we reasonably assume that we don't have to worry about bacteria or other "sanitary" problems. Indeed, what "sanitary" problems could possibly fester in the average family's laundry room? Sure, there may be some loose lint flying around, and maybe the top of the washer is a little sticky from spilled detergent, but I've yet to come across a condition that really needs to be "sanitized." Anyway, who would admit to harboring an unsanitary condition, whatever it is?

Naming a product is very difficult in today's market not only because so many names are already taken but also because so many could be perceived as politically or culturally insensitive. For example, Sambo's restaurant chain changed its name to Season's because African Americans felt that the former name was degrading. I don't think the people who did the renaming realized that Season's was also the brand name for a line of kosher canned foods and condiments, however, which undoubtedly suggested to some people that the restaurants themselves had turned kosher.

Bambeanos would probably be immediately dismissed as a product name in today's climate because of the play on the Italian word for babies, but it was used a couple of decades ago by Colgate-Palmolive for roasted soybean nuts. I can't say the product failed because of the name—the nuts were so hard to chew that I cracked a tooth on one—but I have no idea what a bambeano has to do with soybeans.

Then again, it's always wise to remember that marketing is not an exact science. After all, Banana Republic has nothing to do with clothing, Kodak is a meaningless word that bears no relationship to film (the company's founder thought *K* was a "strong and incisive letter"), and a Macintosh by any other name still might not be a clunky PC, but it sure would be a lot more forgettable.

WHITE HATS AND WARM, FUZZY FEELINGS

Like most people, I've always felt a warm feeling inside when the good guys win. It must go back to my youth, when I'd sit in the balcony of the local movie theater and cheer on the guys who wore the white hats and the gals who had more moxie than a staff sergeant. Often, they were underdogs who had to overcome all sorts of obstacles to triumph in the end.

Americans are eager to embrace people and products that earnestly set out to make a mark and do things a little bit differently. Ben & Jerry's ice cream first came to national attention in the mid-1980s because its owners positioned themselves as do-good Vermont hippies just trying to break into the freezer case against the efforts of established brands such as Häagen-Dazs, which was owned at the time by "big, bad" Pillsbury. Whether you liked hippies or not, you could identify with the little guys taking on the big guy.

It particularly pleases me when minority business people succeed with a product that is outside mainstream American culture. I feel good about the future because I'm reassured that the American Dream is alive and well. And I feel good about the marketplace, which is always enriched by diversity.

David Tsang is the prototypical success story. His House of Tsang line of dry-mix ingredients, specialty sauces, and condiments was an inventive, authentic, and useful offering for chefs experimenting with Chinese cuisine at home. Hormel purchased the House of Tsang in 1992, but David is still tirelessly involved with it. He works with Hormel research and marketing people to develop and refine new products. He never misses an appropriate trade show. Nor is he too proud to continue doing product demonstrations or to make appearances at store openings. He is living proof to me that quality and hard work pay off.

The House of Tsang's product introductions, by the way, have remained consistently excellent under Hormel's ownership, and I'm sure that David's continued presence has been influential. David, unlike some native-born American managers I've known, has not simply taken the money and rested on his laurels.

Thai restaurateur Tommy Tang, with the help of his equally indefatigable wife, Sandi, is another wonderful success story. Besides developing recipes and running his restaurants on both coasts, he writes books, makes videos, and markets sauces, rices, and mixes. Although Tang speaks less-than-perfect English, he has become a popular personality at specialty-food shows. I honestly don't know where he finds the time or energy to accomplish all that he has. Like Tsang, I suspect that Tang will cash in on all his hard work some day, but that he'll continue plugging away promoting his products.

These entrepreneurs seem to really relish what they are doing. Like the guys in the white hats, they seem driven by higher motives than just making a buck. Call me sappy if you must, but it's nice to see the good guys win in the end. It's just a shame that, with all the odds stacked against the little guys and gals, it doesn't happen more often.

WHY DO WE?

- *Reward our poorest customers who buy ten items or less by giving them express lanes while we penalize our best customers by making them wait on insufferably long lines?*

- *Continue to design stores where the items that people buy most frequently—dairy products and bread—are placed the farthest distance from the front door?*

- *Cut margins so close that there's no money left to advertise?* The Club, the device that locks the steering wheels of cars, is as expensive as it is because of all the money spent advertising it. But people buy it in droves because they see it advertised so widely.

- *Make men's shirts with sleeves no longer than 35 inches?* And pants with inseams that leap from 31–32 inches to 33–34 inches? What happens to men with 32–33 inch legs? (You know the ones I'm talking about. Their pants hug their hips or are hiked above their waists.)

- *Advertise "Everything on Sale" and then exclude a whole bunch of merchandise in teensy print on the bottom of our advertising?* It makes consumers distrust everything that we tell them.

- *Continue to baffle consumers with confusing or meaningless standards?* Most shoppers cannot figure out unit prices as they now exist. And who determines what constitutes a normal serving for the nutritional labels? I guarantee you that most consumers eat far more than six potato chips at a sitting, Lay's or not.

• *Charge exorbitant rates for postage and handling of mail-order products?* I've canceled more than a few catalog orders when I've discovered how much an item is really going to cost me.

• *Sell products with descriptions that are meaningless to the average consumer?* Manufacturers may know exactly what they're talking about when they say that a plastic bag will fill a 20-gallon pail, but consumers haven't a clue.

• *Refuse to devise an easy way for consumers to determine the relative strengths of cold and cough remedies?* I've watched people study medicine labels for twenty or thirty minutes trying to determine which product would work best for their particular ailments.

• *Put eight hot dogs in a package, but sell packages of ten buns?*

WORTHLESS POINTS OF DIFFERENCE

As we've discussed, it's essential that you beg, borrow, buy, steal, or concoct a Significant Point of Difference for your product. But there's one more hurdle. It has got to be a point that consumers care about. Take body odor, for example.

Some people maintain that Europeans have a more enlightened attitude toward body odors than North Americans—they just let 'er reek—but I fervently believe that the suppression of noisome emanations is one of the great benefits of living in the time and place that we do. That said, the bad-odor industry certainly has had its fair share of new products that purport to solve problems that really don't exist.

No, I'm not going to retell the story about the ad man who created B.O. (body odor). Like halitosis (bad breath), another copywriter's creation, B.O. was real and ripe for the curing, as far as I'm concerned.

But Nullo, an "edible" deodorant, went too far. The idea was that you pop a Nullo pill, just like you take a vitamin, to suppress body odors for five to seven days. Most people, however, are perfectly content to swipe their underarms as needed and don't feel the need to suppress B.O. for that long a time. (Nullo later repositioned itself as a product for bedridden patients with incontinence problems. It purportedly eliminated the odor of bodily wastes, which was indeed a Significant Point of Difference.)

Then there was Oasis, an antiperspirant/deodorant stick that P&G introduced in 1981 with the "gel" of the deodorant wrapped around the "cream" of the antiperspirant. The gel supposedly acted as a lubricant, preventing underarm hair from being pulled as the stick glided across the underarm. But consumers' regular combination sticks slithered across their hairy pits just fine.

In a similar vein, the mushroom-shaped applicator top of Arrid Extra Dry Shape was supposed to spread the underarm deodorant/antiperspirant better than other products. But the ingredient only came out from small holes in the center of the applicator. Consumers found that they had to swipe their underarms just as often with the mushroom applicator as they did with any other deodorant.

Is the lesson here that people don't want innovative deodorant products? Hardly.

The Mennen Widestick concept has been very successful. That's because you really do need fewer swipes to cover your armpits. Many other deodorant brands now offer wide versions, too.

The lesson is that there are points of difference and there are points of difference. Some are significant. Some are worthless. Don't bother drawing attention to the worthless ones because the consumer will see through them in the end.

Significant Points of Difference are effective solutions to real problems. Worthless Points of Difference are made by products that offer solutions to problems that don't exist.

WHO'S THE ENEMY?

You never know whose applecart you'll be upsetting. If you're introducing a bottled water, for example, you'd think other bottled waters would be your primary enemies. But that depends on how you've positioned the water.

A few years ago, Scotch whisky was the preferred cocktail among the well-to-do. Several advertising campaigns promoted the idea that whisky distilled with pristine Highland water was special. If this were the case, an entrepreneur reasoned, then Americans were ruining their drinks by diluting them with American tap water and ice cubes. He decided to import water from Scotland and sell it to better restaurants and bars, which could then say that their drinks were 100 percent Scotch.

Scotch whisky distributors got wind of the scheme, however, and immediately began bad-mouthing the idea. It won't help Scotch sales at all, they told beverage managers everywhere, to suggest that a Scotch on the rocks mixed with good, ol' American tap water was anything less than 100 percent pure.

The entrepreneur's dream wound up on the rocks.

Remember the golden rule of survivors everywhere: Just because everybody's out to get you doesn't mean you're not paranoid.

X

X SHOULD MARK THE SPOT . . .

. . . where you want the blade to fall. A big, fat X, emblazoned in a bright DayGlo color, should be painted on the back of your neck so that everybody—including the corporate ax wielders—can see it.

Even if you work for a monstrous division of a megalithic subsidiary in a global conglomerate, when you're developing a new product you should think of yourself as an entrepreneur spending your own time and resources. The reason that so many launches from major manufacturers fail is that nobody cares about the product's success as if his mortgage payments depended on it. Be prepared to accept the consequences if things go wrong. And be willing to step forward and prematurely pull the plug on a product that should be killed—even if it's easier to let it die a prolonged death in the marketplace. No, it's not your money. But you've got to act as if it were.

Don't get involved with new products if you're not willing to stick your neck out. Without tremendous risk and courage, there's little chance of success or reward.

Y

YEAH, BUT WHERE'S THE BUSINESS?

A New York retailer I know has a stock response to every scheme, dream, or new product that's pitched to him.

"Yeah," he says, "sounds good. But where's the business? The moola?"

The problem is that there are a million ideas out there that sound great in a presentation or look good in a proposal but don't add up to a viable business. My friend forces the issue. He isn't interested in anything except knowing what his cut of the action will be. And if it can't be demonstrated, he'll politely show you the door. A lot of superficially alluring but fundamentally feeble ideas would have been killed before they did any harm if more marketers took his approach.

Many of these ideas are the result of misinterpretation. Someone sees a niche that really is not there or incorrectly analyzes a trend.

Souper Combos, which the Campbell Soup Company introduced in the mid-1980s, was an attempt to combine a frozen soup and sandwich in one package that could be taken to work or microwaved by the kids at home. The combination of soup and sandwich had

an old-fashioned, grandmotherly ring to it, and it did
well in test.

In assessing the potential for this product, perhaps
Campbell marketers put too much faith in Campbell's
familiar advertising jingle from the 1960s. The jingle
was sung to the tune of "Love and Marriage," a song
that actually was popular a hundred years ago:

> *Soup and sandwich, soup and sandwich*
> *They go together like a horse and carriage*

The problem is, they really don't, no matter how
much they seem like they should. Maybe a soup and a
sandwich was a popular combination when "Love and
Marriage" was a hit song, but it isn't today. I'd be surprised if I've had a soup and sandwich combination
five times during the last decade—which is about as
many times as I've been transported by a horse and

buckboard at the county fair. Souper Combos flopped when it rolled out nationally.

It's easy to see why marketers reading the newspaper in the 1980s might think that Souper Combos would appeal to working moms and dads and their latchkey kids. Three-martini lunches were out; working lunches at the desk were in. Fast-food restaurant fare was not nutritious; soup had a good-for-you aura about it. Kids home from school could just pop a wholesome meal into the microwave just as easily as their parents could at the office.

Those points may look reasonable, but they are so broad and ill-defined as to be meaningless. People make purchases based on more mundane considerations.

First, why would anyone spend a couple of bucks on a combination meal that most people don't eat very often anyway that also:

- Takes up precious freezer space
- Needs to be cooked

Consumers already can make a bowl of soup and throw together a sandwich just about as easily as they could dig out Souper Combos, unwrap its packaging (all eleven pieces of it, which incidentally prompted a environmentalist magazine to give it a "worst product" award), and figure out the proper settings on the microwave. And a fresh sandwich certainly tastes a lot better than a nuked one. Also, some people don't like frozen soups. They like to go through the motions of opening a can, mixing in the water, and perhaps adding some other ingredients. It gives them a feeling of accomplishment.

Second, few people want to tote a frozen meal to

work. They're afraid that it will defrost on the way, which could create a mess. Plus, most people know that food should not be defrosted until just before it's cooked. You could pack it in a thermal bag, but you'd have to buy one. That's an added expense.

Third, once you got Souper Combos to work, where would you store it and prepare it? Yes, some companies have nice, clean refrigerators and gleaming microwaves, but some firms don't have any equipment for employee use at all. The stoves and minirefrigerators that many companies provide are grungy health hazards.

Finally, Souper Combos was too substantial a meal to be an after-school treat for latchkey kids, and it was too light to pass for a full, nutritious dinner if Mom and Dad had to work late.

Campbell reportedly spent $10 million in marketing support as the product faltered in national distribution, but sales kept falling. People tried Souper Combos out of curiosity, but they didn't come back for more. Why? Because people are more than the sum of statistics and trends. In the end, Souper Combos was a product in search of people, not a product that responded to the way that real people lead their lives. In other words, there was no business there. No moola to be had.

YOUTH: HOT BUTTON #8 FOR THE MILLENNIUM

An ever-expanding number of products are aimed directly at kids. Part of this is because both parents are working so kids assume more responsibility for shopping and preparing meals than ever before. They also have more money at their disposal, both for staples such as food as well as for discretionary purchases such as music CDs, jewelry, and personal-care products.

Some marketers have developed kid's versions of adult products. This may not be a good idea for all categories, but it doesn't hurt to have the Crest name on a sweet-tasting toothpaste. Foods such as pizza are also being developed in shapes and flavors that appeal more to younger sensibilities. On the flip side, some marketers are telling adults that it's okay to be seen eating the brands they loved when they were younger (and still secretly crave today). Frosted Flakes is a good example.

The youth market today is a huge niche for just about any product that's not inappropriate, such as tobacco or alcohol. The big-picture story, though, is the effect that technologically savvy kids will have on the way that we market in the near future. I've written elsewhere that microwaves, popular as they are for heating and defrosting, have not fulfilled their promise as a cooking device. I think this will change. Microwave technology will no doubt improve, leading to more versatility as well as greater consistency from model to model. Kids who have been nuking their food since they were in grade school will rise to the challenge. In the not-too-distant future, the kids of today will be teaching their kids how to bake a cake in the microwave.

I'm convinced that the reason why so many experts believe that electronic ordering of products—whether it's via the Internet, interactive TV, or some other gizmo—will be so low is that they can't figure out how to use the technology themselves. That's not the case with kids. Most adults I know joke about how they can't stop their VCRs from flashing 12:00. Most twelve-year-olds think that's pretty lame. They take to the digital world quite readily. They've been using personal computers since preschool, and they are as comfortable with them as we are with the telephone or automobile. They will log on and order products with the same ease that we hop into the car for a trip to the minimall (and imagine what our grandparents would have thought about the way we drive from mall to mall to shop). And don't forget that the technology will become increasingly easy to use, even for baby boomers in their dotage.

One huge implication of online shopping is that it eliminates the need for transportation to the mall. I'm glad my four kids are all grown up and on their own. If they could have ordered whatever they wanted by cruising the virtual, three-dimensional world of a cyberstore, I think I'd still be paying off their bills today. (There will, of course, need to be security restraints and verifications for online shopping, which is a whole new growth area for product development.)

When you think of youth today, think about how their experience will shape the way you market tomorrow. The impact of cyberspace will be just as great as TV was on the current generation of consumers.

And never forget that tomorrow is indeed the day after today.

Z

ZAG WHEN EVERYONE ELSE IS ZIGGING

One way to gain attention in a mature market is to go against the grain.

Original Listerine tastes awful, but it has been the best-selling mouthwash on the market for decades. People believe that Listerine kills the germs that cause bad breath, in fact, *because* it tastes so bad.

What a powerful point of difference! You certainly can't steal market share from Listerine by promoting a product that tastes worse than it does and therefore kills bad-breath germs even more effectively. Listerine's basic positioning is impossible to overcome because it's counterintuitive to begin with. As we discussed in *Alzheimer's, Corporate,* people associate Listerine with bad taste so strongly that Warner-Lambert made a mistake by trying to convince people that it could be a pleasant-tasting toothpaste. At that time, the only version of Listerine tasted so bad that nobody wanted to try the toothpaste.

There's room in the market, of course, for competing mouthwashes that taste better than Listerine. A few decades ago, bright-red Lavoris did a brisk business. More recently, Scope has been a solid number two. And because the market is large enough to support them, some other sweeter-tasting brands, including Listerine's own mint-flavored extensions, also vie for shelf space. Essentially, though, the market consists of Listerine, the heavily advertised, sweeter Scope, and everything else.

How do you make an impact with a new brand in a mature market when the leader is Zagging and everyone else is Zigging? Lump everybody together and Zag again.

That's what Pfizer did. Its Plax purportedly loosens the plaque that contains the germs that can lead to gum disease. It was widely advertised as a dental "rinse" that should be used *before* brushing, not after. It quickly became the number three brand.

You've got to break away from the crowd to make people notice you. Sometimes that means darting ahead, and sometimes it means going in an entirely different direction.

ZEITGEISTS AND THE NEW YORK MINUTE

The Germans use the word *zeitgeist*. It means "the general intellectual, moral, and cultural climate of an era." Once upon a time, it referred to a broad phenomenon that was apparent for a decade or more (the Gay Nineties, the Lost Generation), if not for centuries (the Dark Ages). In this era of media fractionalization and market niches, of instant polls and minute psychodemographic targeting, of split-second MTV images and short attention spans, a zeitgeist is lucky if it lasts the proverbial New York minute.

There are many zeitgeists. They flow and ebb. Generation X, for example. Yuppies. Soccer moms. Here today, gone tomorrow, back in a few years.

Their toys are equally fleeting. Power Rangers. Cigars. The color black. BMWs.

Still, not all marketing zeitgeists are as short-lived as Cajun cooking or as narrowly focused as navel piercing. Some have broad, mass-market appeal. Pepsi-Cola identified its "Generation" more than thirty years ago. By constantly tweaking its image as a more contemporary brand than Coke, it continues to appeal to new generations. And Coke, for all the variety of its images, is still refreshing.

Marketing is certainly not an exact science, nor is product creation and development. It's humbling, in fact, to realize how many innovative products have been the result of pure serendipity or outright mistakes. Ivory Soap, which for decades made a big deal out of its buoyancy, floated because air pockets formed when a batch was left in the mixer too long. Kellogg's Corn Flakes were the result of boiled wheat being left in a baking tin overnight. And when machinery making toilet tissues went haywire and spit out paper with too many layers, the Scott Paper Company turned lemons into lemonade by creating the paper towel.

Do such fortuitous mistakes still happen today? You bet. But they can only happen in an atmosphere where people are encouraged to think creatively, to experiment, to be willing to make mistakes, to spot an opportunity where other people see failure. Unfortunately, because of all the downsizing at corporations, the employees who are left behind have a hard enough time keeping up with their day-to-day work. There's little time left to think creatively or thoroughly. Creative developers must have the time to noodle and doodle, to make mistakes and travel down wrong paths.

Innovation is undoubtedly 99 percent perspiration and 1 percent inspiration. It has become very costly to develop truly innovative products, and most companies unfortunately no longer seem willing, or able, to make such risky investments.

In many ways, it's really up to individuals like you, whether you are within a large organization or on your own, to think creatively and persevere. And that often means making mistakes.

There is no better path to success, I believe, than by learning from your losses. History is filled with great men and women who endured setback after setback. Abraham Lincoln failed in business twice, lost eight campaigns for various elective offices, suffered the death of his sweetheart, and overcame a nervous breakdown before he became one of our most revered leaders. The history of marketing is likewise filled with notable examples of people and products that have rebounded from despair and disaster. We should respect our losers even as we admire our winners. Never forget that we have at least as much to learn from failure as we do from success.

As Lao-tzu said, "Failure is an opportunity."

Pay attention to history with the same devotion that you track trends. Although product cycles move much more quickly nowadays, and the pace will only quicken, there's very often a parallel in the past that will give you the grounding you need to survive.

As George Santayana said, "Those who cannot remember the past are condemned to repeat it."

Finally, don't give up.

As Julia Child said, "You can't turn a sow's ear into a Veal Orloff, but you can do something very good with a sow's ear."

And if you're still not convinced that innovative, successful new products are often the result of previous failure, come up to visit me at the New Products Showcase in Ithaca, New York. I'll argue my case tangibly with thousands of examples of misconceived, misbegotten, and plain, old mistaken products that prove, to paraphrase Euripides, that second thoughts, indeed, are best.

INDEX

Accents Potpourri Glass Cleaner, 26
adult-incontinence pads, 168
advertising, 13–15
  agencies, 12–13, 183
  awards for, 188–89
  image, beverage marketing and,
    107–9
  labeling regulations and, 134
  product price and, 215
Advertising Age, 188–89
Advil, 127
Afri Cola, 129
Agree shampoo, 98
Alka-Seltzer, 188–89
American Brands, Jergens Liquid
  Soap, 8
American culture, 151, 213
American Dental Association, 130
American Tobacco, 180
America Online, 14–15, 194
Amoco gasoline, 75
Amway, 157
Anchor Brewing, 16
Angel Skin, 97
Anheuser-Busch, 15–16, 117
animal testing, 61
"anti-advertising," 108
Arizona Iced Tea, 187, 198
  Freez-A-Pops, 27
Arm & Hammer toothpaste, 131
Arrid Extra Dry Shape, 217
Ass Kickin' Cajun Hot Sauce, 199
automobile industry, 62, 173
Avert Virucidal Tissues, 181, 182

bad-odor industry, 216–18
Baker's Select Bread Mix, 31–32
Baker Tom's cat food, 195–96

Bambeanos, 212
Banana Republic, 212
Barnum's Animal Crackers, 78–79
Bayer
  Aspirin, 186–87
  Select analgesics, 186, 187
BBQ Buddies, 109–10
Beano, 170
beer
  advertising, 13–14
  nonalcoholic, 106
  sales and profits, 15–17
benefits vs. features, 21–22
Ben-Gay Aspirin, 23
Ben & Jerry's ice cream, 81–82,
  212–13
  Rain Forest Crunch, 177
Benetton™, 179
Bernays, Edward L., 180
Betacam recorders, 112
Betty Crocker, 65
beverage industry
  image advertising, 107–9
  "New Age," 73, 75, 77, 195
Bigelow Constant Comment Sparkling
  Iced Tea, 195
Big Mac, 125
Bird's Eye Soda Burst, 148
blacks, 150, 211
body odors, 216–18
Boeing 777 aircraft, xvi
Bone Sucking Sauce marinades, 199
Borden
  Cracker Jack Extra Fresh Popping
    Corn, 86
  Creamettes, 207
Boston Market, 36
Bounty Select-A-Size, 163–64